The Kid on the Sandlot

The Kid
on the Sandlot:

Congress and Professional Sports,

1910-1992

Stephen R. Lowe

Bowling Green State University Popular Press
Bowling Green, OH 43403

Sports and Culture

General Editors
Douglas Noverr
Lawrence Ziewacz

Other books in the series:

The Sports Immortals:
Deifying the American Athlete
Peter Williams

Hunting and Fishing for Sport:
Commerce, Controversy, Popular Culture
Richard Hummel

Cricket for Americans:
Playing and Understanding the Game
Tom Melville

Baseball in 1889:
Players vs. Owners
Daniel M. Pearson

Copyright © 1995 Bowling Green State University Popular Press

Library of Congress Catalog Card Number: 94-79195

ISBN: 0-87972-675-X Clothbound
0-87972-676-8 Paperback

Cover type and design by Dumm Art, illustration by Gary Dumm

For

Kimberly

"Baseball is the kid on the sandlot and the shirt-sleeve fan in the stands; baseball is the sports writer in the press box and the sports pages he turns out. Baseball is hotdogs and peanuts; arguments and enthusiasm..."

—Ford Frick, 1951

Preface

In *Winning Is the Only Thing: Sports in America Since 1945*, Randy Roberts and James Olson observe that before World War II sports "knew its place in American culture" as a "pastime, diversion, leisure" activity that provided "relief from the real things of the world" such as "wars . . . politics, religion, work . . . and family"; however, after the war sports became a "national obsession" that replaced work, family, and religion as the central focus in many people's lives (xi-xii). Unfortunately, Roberts and Olson are correct in their assessment. Sports are no longer mere pastimes, but multi-million-dollar industries that have a tremendous influence on American life. For this reason, over the last 40 years the U.S. Congress has developed an important and interesting relationship with the world of professional sports.

Since the 1951 investigation into organized baseball, Congress has held dozens of hearings on the subject of professional sports. The issues that have grabbed Congress's attention are organized baseball's position under the antitrust laws, the creation of a federal boxing commission, professional sports broadcasting, league mergers, and franchise relocations.

This book will examine the checkered relationship that has developed between Congress and professional sports. At times Congress has been quite friendly to professional sports, particularly to organized baseball; at other times, Congress has been less friendly. In either case, the public image of the professional sport involved has been a decisive factor in Congress's behavior. Although it is a relationship of which most sports fans are unaware, it is one that has greatly influenced professional sports. In light of the huge role that professional sports play in American life, we can assume that Congress's involvement with professional sports will expand in the future.

* * *

A number of teachers and scholars have influenced me over the past ten years. Throughout my undergraduate years at Olivet

Nazarene University, Professor Bill Isaacs provided encouragement and valuable counsel. I thank Professor Charles Alexander, my graduate advisor at Ohio University for suggesting the relationship between Congress and professional sports as a potential seminar topic in the winter of 1989 and for directing it, finally, to a doctoral dissertation. Beyond his insightful criticisms and advice on this project, I am grateful to Professor Alexander for providing me an example of the consummate teacher and scholar. I thank Professor Alonzo Hamby for giving me the opportunity to do graduate work at Ohio University and for serving on my examining committee. I also appreciate the time and help given by the other members of my examining committee, Professors Marvin Fletcher and Alexander Prisley.

My father and mother, Stephen and Arlene Lowe, deserve more thanks for the faith and guidance they have given me over the years than I could possibly put into words. They taught me by example and are the two wisest people I know. My sister, Robin, and her husband, Ken, my good friend Mark Fryar, and my uncle, Jerry Harms, have been important sources of motivation and encouragement. Also, I thank my wife, Kimberly, who retyped the manuscript and improved it at a number of points. Of course, my debt to her goes far deeper than her work on this book. She not only puts up with me, but brings more love, happiness, and support into my life than she knows. Finally, I am thankful to God, whose grace makes all things possible.

Contents

Introduction

In the post-World War II era, committees of the U.S. Congress expanded the scope of their inquiries.[1] One American institution that has received a great deal of attention from various congressional committees since 1951 is professional sports. Except for dedicated sports fans and a growing number of scholars committed to the study of sports, the relationship between Congress and professional sports is little known. Yet, Congress has exerted a considerable amount of leverage over professional sports, particularly with regard to antitrust exemptions, and has seriously influenced professional baseball, football, basketball, boxing, and, to a lesser degree, ice hockey.

The few scholarly works treating the relationship between Congress and professional sports have done so only in an indirect manner. A number of excellent anthologies, such as Roger G. Noll's *Government and the Sports Business* (1974), Arthur T. Johnson and James H. Frey's *Government and Sport: The Public Policy Issues* (1985), and Paul D. Staudohar and James A. Mangan's *The Business of Professional Sports* (1991), provide bits and pieces of the history of that relationship, but these studies are more concerned with the general problem of sports and contemporary public policy. Another genre of sports literature has dealt specifically with the subject of professional sports and the law. Representative of this group are Lionel Sobel's *Professional Sports and the Law* (1977), Robert C. Berry and Glenn M. Wong's two-volume study *Law and the Business of the Sports Industries* (1986), and Warren Freedman's *Professional Sports and Anti-Trust* (1987). While each of these works offers solid indirect treatment of Congress and professional sports, a full-length examination devoted solely to the relationship between these two institutions has yet to surface.[2]

Despite this gap in scholarly sports literature, a consensus has developed among many sports scholars regarding the relationship between Congress and professional sports: Prior to 1965, Congress generally viewed professional sports as idyllic, innocent games that happened to be businesses; since 1965, Congress has increasingly treated professional sports primarily as big businesses that require a

1

watchful eye and occasional congressional intervention.[3] My research confirms this interpretation as a basically sound, yet excessively broad, explanation of the history of Congress and professional sports. Indeed, the public images projected by the *individual* professional sports have determined their treatment by Congress. It is true that professional sports as a group underwent a revision in their public images in the mid-1960s. Franchise relocations, television package contracts, players' unions, strikes, and publicized salaries all contributed to the creation of a new image of professional sports as big business.

Yet, Congress has never treated professional sports as a monolith. Each professional sport has its own tradition, place, and image in American life. At one end of the spectrum is professional boxing, which has seen its popularity rise and fall throughout the 20th century, but its image has most often been of a sport only a step ahead of the law and abolitionist reformers.[4] Thus, boxing has been the subject of scathing inquiries by congressional committees —and the sport most often considered for federal regulation. On the other end of the spectrum sits organized baseball—"our game," the "American game," and the "national pastime."[5] To be sure, baseball's place in the overall American sports scene has diminished, but the sport's success in projecting an image of a game played by kids on sandlots across the country has continued to protect organized baseball's privileged position under the antitrust laws.

In their historical relationship to Congress, professional football and basketball are located somewhere between organized baseball and professional boxing. Professional football, of course, has not benefited from the patriotic nostalgia that has blessed organized baseball, but it has reaped the most profits from network television. In fact, the meteoric rise of professional football in the 1960s was primarily the result of its marriage to the television industry.[6] Huge profits, coupled with a lack of a protective romantic shell, have created an image of professional football as a big business that neither needs nor deserves protection from Congress.

Professional basketball, the one sport with a clear right to be called the "American game," inasmuch as it was unquestionably invented in the United States, nonetheless has relatively little tradition as a professional sport.[7] Thus, when professional basketball sought congressional approval to merge two competing leagues in 1971, it was turned away. As for professional ice hockey, Congress has dealt with that sport only on a marginal basis. Congress, presumably a reflection of the American public, has always treated professional hockey as a Canadian sport played mostly by Canadians (and by increasing numbers of Europeans) in the United States.

I am not suggesting that the only important factor in the relationship between Congress and professional sports is the individual sport's public image. Each congressional hearing or investigation has its own rationale. Yet, the one common denominator that influences congressional treatment is the image and perceived tradition, prestige (or lack thereof) of a particular professional sport.

The organization of this book is roughly chronological, but essentially topical. Following the chapter 1 history of Congress and professional sports prior to World War II, the emphasis of the book is on the period since World War II considered in three sections. The first section discusses the positions that the various professional sports have held in relation to the antitrust laws, the anomalous position of baseball, and the question of federal regulation of boxing. The second section is devoted to Congress's treatment of professional sports broadcasting, with chapters on the decline of minor league baseball in the 1950s and Congress's efforts to deal with that problem; professional football's 1961 exemption from the antitrust laws for the purpose of forming package television contracts; and to the television blackout controversy of 1972–75. The third section deals with league mergers and franchise relocations, the successful merger of the National Football League and the American Football League in 1966, the failed merger of the National Basketball League and American Basketball Association in 1972, and the controversy over sports franchise relocations in the early 1980s.

The focus is on the events that precipitated the various congressional hearings and investigations, the issues and positions staked out in a given hearing or investigation, and the major personalities involved, both in Congress and the professional sports world. Thus, the purpose of this study is not to produce an exhaustive catalog or listing of everything that has involved the two parties. Rather, the purpose is to provide a concise, interpretive treatment of the relationship between Congress and professional sports—an inquiry that will contribute to the growing body of scholarly sports literature as well as illuminate an important aspect of 20th-century American life.

Chapter 1

A New-Found Credibility?
Congress and Professional Sports, 1910–45

Congress's interest in professional sports did not really bloom until after World War II, although the federal government did concern itself with the world of sports in the years before the war. One of the best-known encounters was the involvement of President Theodore Roosevelt with collegiate football in 1905. Big-time football, still confined to college campuses during this era, was characterized by exceptionally high levels of enthusiasm and violence. Deaths resulting from football competition were fairly common; serious injuries had become an accepted part of the game. The president's own son played at Harvard and had suffered severe bruises and a black eye while on the freshman squad.[1] By the eve of the 1905 season, public concern over the violence in collegiate football had reached such a level that President Roosevelt summoned an elite group of academicians, including representatives from Harvard, Yale, and Princeton, to the White House for lunch to discuss reforming the game.[2]

The *Washington Post* reported that though no definite conclusions had been reached at the luncheon, the president had successfully started "the ball rolling" toward reform.[3] The *New York Times* applauded the president for taking "up another question of vital interest to the American people."[4] President Roosevelt did, if nothing else, give the ball of reform a push, and the rules of collegiate football were modified to reduce injuries and appease public opinion. President Roosevelt's White House luncheon was only the first of a number of highly publicized attempts by the federal government to exercise leverage over the sports world.

Another brush between the federal government and sports involved organized baseball. The national pastime, which baseball clearly was in the 1920s, was shaken to its foundation by a scandal in September 1924. In the midst of a tight pennant race, at least one

New York Giants player was involved in attempting to bribe the Philadelphia Phillies into throwing an insurance game to the Giants.[5] Like the 1919 Black Sox scandal, the 1924 scandal was shrouded in mystery and confusion, but in the fall of 1924 American League President Ban Johnson was not convinced that Baseball Commissioner Kenesaw Mountain Landis had conducted a thorough investigation of the affair.[6]

Although there had been no federal probe into the 1919 World Series, Johnson and Barney Dreyfuss, president of the Pittsburgh Pirates, began clamoring for a federal investigation into the problem in order to restore baseball's integrity. Johnson even suggested calling off the 1924 World Series and added, "Baseball is the national game of our country and it must be protected by the government. I will insist upon an investigation by the Federal Judiciary." Commissioner Landis responded that "gentleman clothed with responsibility" should "keep their shirts on."[7]

At bottom, Johnson's threats to involve the federal government were aimed more at Commissioner Landis, his archenemy, than at organized baseball's integrity.[8] Still, the episode displayed the willingness of some people within a professional sport to look to the federal government in time of crisis.

However, these episodes in the sports world did not directly involve the national legislative authority. The first major meeting between Congress and professional sports occurred in the summer of 1910 as a result of the storm brewing over prizefight films. The issue became a controversy following the heavyweight fight between the "white hope," Jim Jeffries, and the notorious black champion, Jack Johnson, held on July 4, 1910, in Reno, Nevada. The fight had been promoted as a battle not so much between two boxers as between two races, and support for the two fighters divided distinctly along racial lines. Johnson, despised by many whites because he consistently overstepped the boundaries that a "good nigger" was supposed to observe, was in his prime as a fighter, while Jeffries was pursuing an ill-advised comeback from retirement. When the fight was over, Johnson was still standing after slowly and deliberately beating Jeffries to a pulp. Another white hope had turned into disappointment, and much of white America was frustrated and outraged at Johnson and what some considered his arrogant behavior.

Arthur Ruhl, writing for the popular magazine *Collier's*, called the fight "a pretty sad affair," but added that Johnson had "fought and vanquished a brave opponent cleanly and like a brave man."[9] Other observers throughout the country did not view the fight in such a favorable light, and took to the streets in a display of rioting that touched a number of communities, particularly in the South. In Uvalda, Georgia, for example, a white mob killed three blacks and wounded five more, and in Washington, D.C., several blacks fatally stabbed two whites.[10]

After the rioting ceased, Congress worried about the potential for further riots if the film of the fight were shown in theaters across the country. Many local leaders, such as Mayor Louis Schwab of Cincinnati, banned the film; in all, 15 states and the District of Columbia passed laws banning its showing.[11] Film was the medium through which most boxing fans witnessed major fights before the advent of television; naturally, some congressmen feared a repeat of the riots that immediately followed the Johnson-Jeffries fight.

The U.S. House of Representatives' Committee on Interstate and Foreign Commerce held hearings in May 1910 and February 1911 to debate the potential danger of disseminating prizefight films. Congress, of course, could deal with the problem only on an interstate basis; indeed, the proposed legislation that initiated the hearings attempted to make it a crime to transport across state lines "any picture or description of any prizefight or encounter of pugilists."[12]

Oscar Nielson, better known as "Battling" Nelson during his days in the ring, was the most colorful witness called to testify during the relatively brief hearings. Nelson testified during the session of May 17, 1910, and proved a stalwart defender of professional boxing. Nelson opposed the ban because "Next to baseball, boxing is the most legitimate sport that we know of, if not the most." He further argued that the sport should be encouraged in schools and athletic clubs around the country because it was "the most manly of all athletic sports" and provided the "greatest exercise in the world . . . to guard against sickness and to save on doctors' bills." Nelson also believed that the spread of the art of pugilism would reduce the need for violent weapons such as guns and knives. Finally, Nelson took his highest ground by arguing that boxing promoted moral character among the nation's youth, as it discouraged young men from "smoke," "chew," and "drink."[13]

Representative Thetus Sims of Tennessee reminded Nelson that the proposed legislation would ban not the manly sport but only the interstate transportation of fight films. Representative Sims also disclosed the racial motivation of the bill by suggesting a compromise that would ban only films of interracial fights.[14] Interestingly, the record of the hearings makes only the slightest reference to the fact that the proposed legislation was racially driven.

Both professional boxing and Battling Nelson dodged any knockout punch for two years following the calling of the hearings, partly because the film of the Johnson-Jeffries fight was of such poor quality that its success was self-limiting.[15] But in the summer of 1912 another interracial fight involving champion Jack Johnson and the latest white hope, Jim Flynn, provided the impetus necessary to carry the anti-fight-film legislation into law. Two Southern congressmen, Representative Seaborn A. Roddenberry of Georgia and Senator Furnifold Simmons of North Carolina, introduced bills in their respective houses to get a legal ban on the interstate transportation of fight films. Senator Simmons was initially more successful than his partner; the Senate passed the legislation on June 15, 1912, anticipating the Johnson-Flynn bout slated for July 4.[16] The House, however, failed to pass the measure before July 4.[17]

The bout between Johnson and Flynn was fought on schedule in Las Vegas, New Mexico. As he had done two years earlier, Johnson easily crushed the white hope. One account reported that at one point during the fight, Johnson talked to ringsiders while Flynn "was ineffectually hitting his midsection."[18] The perception of some was that once again Johnson had not only defeated the white race, but had insulted it in the process.

During an address on the floor of the House on July 19, Representative Roddenberry described the fight as "perhaps the grossest instance of base fraud and bogus effort at a fair fight between a Caucasian brute and an African biped beast that has ever taken place."[19] Moments after Roddenberry finished his speech, the House, by a voice vote, passed the measure banning interstate transportation of fight films, and President William H. Taft signed the bill into law on July 31.[20]

As Randy Roberts has pointed out, white America finally found a white hope whom Johnson could not defeat. In fact, it was the U.S. Congress that delivered the knockout blow to Johnson's career with the passage of the Mann Act in 1910.[21] The Mann Act, or the White Slave Traffic Act, made it illegal to transport women across state lines for the purpose of engaging in immoral behavior. Congress passed the Progressive law in response to the public's fear that many foreign and native-born women were being lured or forced into a complex, evil prostitution ring. In order to eliminate any potential loopholes, the law covered both commercial and voluntary vice, but in 98% of the 2,801 cases prosecuted between 1910 and 1920 the defendants were involved in commercialized prostitution.[22] Though he was among the other 2%, Johnson was a prime target once Congress passed the Mann Act because he was notorious for traveling with one or more prostitutes, usually white.

In 1913 a federal grand jury successfully prosecuted Johnson under the Mann Act on eleven counts ranging from debauchery to crimes against nature.[23] Johnson was convicted by an all-white jury and sentenced to one year in prison. Rather than serve his sentence, the heavyweight champ jumped bail and fled to Europe. After losing his championship in 1915 to Jess Willard, Johnson ceased to be a major concern to Congress and white America in general.

As for the antifight film law, it was being widely violated by the 1920s. Congress tried to toughen its penalties, but that bill failed and the original antifight film law remained on the books until a new Congress, in a new boxing era, decided to reconsider the law in 1939.[24] By then boxing had a spruced up image, and all 48 states had legalized the sport.[25]

Hearings were held May 25–26, 1939, by a subcommittee of the Senate Committee on Interstate Commerce on S. 2047, a bill to overturn the 1912 law. The bill was the work of Senator Warren K. Barbour of New Jersey, an ex-boxer who had once held the national amateur heavyweight title and had himself been a leading white hope in his youth.[26] The three-man subcommittee, chaired by Senator Ernest Lundeen of Minnesota, included Senator Edwin C. Johnson of Colorado and Senator Charles W. Tobey of New Hampshire. The members of the subcommittee seem to have made up their minds before the hearings began. At the outset Senator Johnson heralded the proposed bill as one that was "very much . . . in the interest of the common people, people who would not have an opportunity to see a real champion in action."[27] Senator Tobey concurred, adding that Congress should take "dead laws off the statute books."[28]

Like the 1912 hearings, the brief 1939 inquiry was highlighted by the colorful testimony of an ex-boxer, in this case Jack Dempsey. Dempsey, a sports hero of the 1920s second only to Babe Ruth, drew a large crowd into the hearing room. One newspaper reported that "a bevy of Senate Office Building girl stenographers and touring sightseers crowded the public hearing and goggled at the former champion."[29] Congressmen quickly learned that a sports hero could turn an ordinary legislative hearing into a thriving public forum; Dempsey would not be the last well-known sports figure to testify in Congress.

Dempsey, of course, supported the legislation to repeal the antifight film law. He sang the praises of the "greatest sport in the world," one that allowed "two he-men" to "get up into the ring and fight." The sport was also more genteel in 1939 than in 1912, according to Dempsey. In the "old days" the "rougher the fighter, the better," suggested Dempsey, but now "the cleaner you are and more gentlemanly you are the further you go." Senator Lundeen agreed with Dempsey's analysis. Boxing, he said, "has passed beyond the pale now of mere slugging matches." Indeed, one interesting theme of the hearings was the "scientific" nature of the sport, an aspect of the game not emphasized in the 1912 hearings. Dempsey also testified that he believed he had lost close to $2 million in personal income as a result of the anti-fight-film law. As for racial concerns, he assured the subcommittee that they were "living in a different age and a different era" than the one in which the bill banning fight films was passed. The anti-fight-film law, concluded Dempsey, should be "knocked out."[30]

Other less-colorful witnesses also made persuasive arguments favoring repeal of the 1912 legislation. Neville Miller, president of the National Association of Broadcasters, wondered what would become of the anti-fight-film law when television arrived. Miller reminded the members of the subcommittee that the new communications medium was just on the horizon, and urged a repeal of the 1912 law.[31] Theofiel Wageman, director of the New Hampshire National Youth Administration's Boys Program, testified that the sport was not harmful to the nation's youth, while several theater owners characterized the anti-fight-film law as a "joke" and a "farce" because it was so easy to break.[32]

The imminence of television and the ineffectiveness of the 1912 law were persuasive arguments but secondary to the perception that racial tension had eased throughout the country and that the sport had generally improved its public image. That boxing's image had been improved was due in large part to the eclipse of Jack Johnson and the rise of such boxers as Jack Dempsey and Gene Tunney in the 1920s and Joe Louis in the 1930s. These men did a lot to make the country forget about Jack Johnson and to create a new image for the heavyweight champion and boxing in general.

Dempsey, for example, related to the subcommittee that he had made visits to orphanages to urge youths "not to drink or smoke until after 21 years old, until their bodies had been developed."[33] Such comments and behavior were in step with Dempsey's public image as a man of conservative values, patriotism, and modest temper. These characteristics have led one biographer to suggest that Dempsey may have provided a better symbol for the 1920s than either Henry Ford or Charles Lindbergh.[34]

More importantly for the demise of the anti-fight-film law, Joe Louis, the current heavyweight title-holder, was a champion of whom white America approved. Referring to Louis, Fred J. Saddy, secretary of the State Athletic Commission of Wisconsin, told the subcommittee that "these colored champions . . . conduct themselves very well."[35] Indeed, in many ways Joe Louis was left with the task of living down the legacy of Jack Johnson, which he did by not challenging racial taboos and conducting himself with dignity and modesty in public.[36] In later years Louis would write about the things that a boxer could not do, such as "keep late hours . . . drink . . . smoke . . . [or] overeat."[37] Fortunately for professional boxing, Dempsey and Louis represented everything that Jack Johnson did not.

Thus, the subcommittee reported the bill to repeal the anti-fight-film law favorably to the full committee. Thanks to Joe Louis, the subcommittee could say that the racial tension characterizing boxing in 1912 existed no longer. Moreover, the committee concluded that the sport had gained a "new-found credibility" and through its films could provide "wholesome entertainment that many less wealthy are deprived of." The members of the subcommittee also cited the imminence of television as a reason to reconsider the anti-fight-film law. Finally, the fact that no witness opposed repealing the 1912 law and that the law was being violated almost at will led the subcommittee members to support unanimously legislation to repeal the anti-fight-film law.[38] Such action was taken on June 13, 1939, by the Senate and on June 21, 1940, by the House of Representatives. President Franklin D. Roosevelt signed the bill into law on June 29, 1940.[39]

The anti-fight-film legislation and its repeal represent the only significant involvement of Congress in professional sports in the pre-World War II era. In some ways, this early meeting differed from the numerous congressional hearings on professional sports that would occur in the post-World War II era. For example, race relations, central to the fight-film controversy, would be mostly absent from issues involving Congress and professional sports in later years. Also, Congress would never again concern itself with motion pictures and professional sports, although it would become heavily involved in broadcasting issues, of which it could be argued that the fight-film controversy was the first. Finally, the hearings of 1912 and 1939 were much more concise, less publicized, and more efficient than the dozens of hearings that Congress would hold on professional sports issues in the post-World War II era.

In many other ways, however, the 1912 and 1939 hearings forecast post-World War II developments. Although race did not prove to be a determining factor in later hearings (it played a minor role in the basketball league merger hearings in 1971–72), the factor of the public image of particular sports did figure in a major way in later hearings, as had been the case in the fight-film controversy. The records of the 1912 and 1939 hearings demonstrate clearly that the image of professional boxing affected congressional behavior. In this case, of course, race and public image were very much intertwined; but although the factor of race would diminish, public image would remain the constant determining factor and would become intertwined with other issues, such as the reserve clause, franchise relocations, and broadcasting policies.

Congressmen and professional sports interests realized early the popular appeal and propaganda value of professional sports stars. Battling Nelson and Jack Dempsey were the first two of many professional athletes who would draw spectators into hearing rooms in the same way that they drew customers to the arenas and stadia. Indeed, when the monumental investigation into organized baseball was called to order in 1951, Congress and organized baseball were playing on a field that had been constructed before World War II.

Part I

Baseball, Boxing, and Monopoly

Chapter 2

As American as the Constitution, 1951

On July 11, 1949, the House Judiciary Committee, under the direction of its chairman, Emanuel Celler of New York, created subcommittee number 5 or, as it came to known, the Subcommittee on Anti-Trust and Monopoly. The purpose of the subcommittee—one of many that grew out of the Legislative Reorganization Act of 1946—was to study monopoly power in postwar American industry. The 1946 congressional reform law effectively reduced the number of full committees in both houses of Congress, but increased the number of subcommittees over the two decades or so following its passage.[1] Another by-product of the 1946 reform act was that the size of congressional staffs more than doubled on the average.[2] The increase in subcommittees and staffs allowed Congress to become more specialized and junior members to become more active in the legislative process.[3]

However, in 1949 Emanuel Celler was one of the most active and powerful members of Congress. Celler first entered Congress in 1923 as a Democratic representative from the Brooklyn, New York, district and by 1949 he had worked his way to the powerful chairmanship of the House Judiciary Committee. (The majority party, usually the Democrats in this period, appointed full committee and subcommittee chairs on the basis of seniority and a congressman's interests and preference.)[4] And Celler was not afraid to use his power during his tenure as chairman from 1949 to 1972. Under his leadership the House Judiciary Committee grew in influence and after his retirement its power decreased.[5] Celler was a committee chairman who led with an "iron hand in a velvet glove."[6] During his tenure, the Judiciary Committee faced such volatile issues as gun control, abortion, prayer in schools, and busing, besides organized baseball's antitrust exemption.

Celler appointed himself the chairman of the Subcommittee on Anti-Trust and Monopoly. He was quite powerful as chairman of both the full Judiciary Committee and the new subcommittee inasmuch as

15

he purposely assigned vague jurisdictions to the other subcommittees so that he could guide important bills and issues to his sub-committee.[7] Such power was not atypical in these years; indeed, the period from 1947 to 1964 was one of extraordinarily strong, secure, and stable committee chairs.[8] Senior congressmen expected junior members to defer to chairmen who shouldered such responsibilities as setting the agenda of committees, appointing members to subcommittees, referring bills to subcommittees, deciding what pending measures should be considered and when, calling and presiding over committee meetings, deciding whether to hold hearings and when, approving the list of scheduled witnesses, and authorizing staff studies.[9] Congressional reforms in the early 1970s chipped away much of the committee chair's influence, but in the 1950s he wielded tremendous power. All of this points to the fact that Celler must accept the ultimate responsibility for the calling, conduct, and results of the 1951 investigation into organized baseball.

His contemporaries seemed to agree, because Celler immediately felt heat as Americans learned of his subcommittee's planned probe into the national pastime. "Then came the baseball inquiry . . . the Hornet's Nest," he wrote in his autobiography. "If I thought storms had broken furiously over my head before, I knew better when these [baseball] hearings started."[10] Celler's subcommittee quickly gained a reputation as the post-World War II trust watchdog, if not trustbuster. But most Americans agreed that if any monopoly was justified, it was organized baseball's. Nevertheless, Celler's subcommittee moved into its baseball investigation in the summer of 1951 following hearings on the aluminum, steel, and newspaper print industries.

Celler claimed that the hearings were scheduled because the subcommittee had received complaints from disgruntled ballplayers and because three bills designed to give baseball statutory antitrust exemption had been introduced into Congress. If Celler did receive numerous written complaints from ballplayers, he failed to leave them to posterity.[11] He later wrote that the investigation would give the subcommittee the "unique opportunity to study anti-trust policies as applied to a self-regulated industry." And Celler added, "that Organized Baseball today is 'big-business' cannot be denied."[12] As for the three exemption bills, they were introduced by Representative Wilbur D. Mills of Arkansas, Representative Melvin Price of Illinois, and Representative A.S. Herlong of Florida (a former president of the Florida State League), primarily because organized baseball was coming under heavy fire from antitrust suits spawned by the Mexican League controversy.

The court cases developed when eighteen major-league players "jumped" their contracts with organized baseball franchises to play in the rival Mexican League. This represented a blatant violation of organized baseball's hallowed reserve clause. From 1879 to 1975 baseball operated with a contractual clause that "reserved" or bound a player to a club as long as that club wanted to exercise its option to sign him to another contract. The club could renew his contract when it expired, trade him, or release him, but it was the *club's* decision, not the *player's*. Celler referred to the reserve clause as the "center of the storm," and it would prove to be the most important link that joined Congress to the affairs of organized baseball.

By crossing the border to play for bigger dollars in the Mexican League, players had ignored the reserve clause, and commissioner of baseball Albert B. "Happy" Chandler decided to punish the players by banning them from the major leagues for five years. That was in 1946. When the players quickly attempted to return to the major leagues and ran up against Chandler's ban, they resorted to the federal courts, arguing that the owners were engaged in a monopoly that threatened their livelihood of playing professional baseball. Relying on the 1922 *Federal League* case, the courts ruled in favor of major league baseball. Having won the court battle, Chandler lifted the ban for the 1949 season to "temper justice with mercy," as he put it.[13]

The most famous of these cases was that of Danny Gardella.[14] Gardella's case was unique in that he was only a reserve jumper and not a contract jumper. Also, Gardella did win a victory of sorts when a U.S. Court of Appeals reversed an earlier dismissal of his case and sent it back to the federal district court judge for trial. This trial, however, would have taken months, and Gardella was anxious to play in the 1949 season. Thus, Gardella sought a preliminary injunction to allow him to play in 1949. The injunction was never granted, and it was this fact that prompted Chandler to lift the ban and settle Gardella's—and other players'—matters out of court. The out-of-court settlement seemed to satisfy everyone involved, and the antitrust litigation was dropped.

The competition from the Mexican League and the antitrust suits that it created were the most important forces that brought Congress and organized baseball together. Besides the reserve clause, the subcommittee was interested in other monopolistic practices of the game, such as franchise distribution and territorial rights, the farm system, and the powers of the commissioner. Chairman Celler took pains to assure the public that the subcommittee was "gunning for no one, [but was] just trying to . . . help baseball against itself."[15] Celler also wanted to make it clear that "the witnesses that have been called have been invited, not subpoenaed," and that while President Harry S Truman was initially concerned, he now "wholeheartedly" endorsed the subcommittee's probe.[16]

For its part, organized baseball put a positive spin on the investigation as well. In a speech at the annual Hall of Fame festivities in Cooperstown, Ford Frick declared that "a better game will come out of the hearings. . . . The committee will clear away the mists and open a new highway for baseball through the years ahead." And in case the subcommittee had anything else in mind, Frick reminded the audience that the game was as "American as the Constitution" and could not "be hurt, for baseball belongs not to us but baseball belongs to all of you people, to the small business man, to the little kids in the street, to the shut-ins in hospitals."[17]

Nearly a week before the hearings convened, the press learned that Ty Cobb was scheduled to be the "lead off" witness.[18] The subcommittee members believed that player representatives for the major leagues also "must be called" to speak for players at large.[19] There was also some question as to whether the hearings would be televised, but Celler and the rest of the subcommittee members decided that permitting television cameras would be unwise, because it was likely viewers would be exposed to only controversial slices of the hearings rather than the entire process. Instead, the subcommittee decided to allow photographers into the hearing room, but with the limit of one photograph per photographer per day.[20]

With the Mexican League episode fresh in their minds, the members of the House Subcommittee on the Study of Monopoly Power convened on July 30, 1951, to discuss the practices and structure of organized baseball. The *Sporting News* reported that there was standing room only in the hearing room that July morning as Ty Cobb led off for organized baseball. Though 64 years old, Cobb appeared in excellent physical condition for his sole appearance on Capitol Hill.

Throughout his testimony, the former star firmly defended the game and particularly the reserve clause. He argued that the elimination of the reserve clause would lead to a maldistribution of player strength and thus a decreasing level of competition.[21] It is interesting to note that Cobb defended the reserve clause on virtually the same ground on which it was being attacked. According to Cobb, the reserve clause prevented a different type of monopoly, one based on franchise wealth. Thus, the reserve clause could be considered either monopolistic or antimonopolistic, depending on how a person chose to view it. Cobb's defense had been the primary argument used to support the reserve clause's creation in 1879, and although he was the first to use that argument in behalf of the status quo in a congressional hearing, he was certainly not the last.[22]

Cobb also declared that baseball was a sport, not a big business needing governmental regulation.[23] He concluded by telling the subcommittee that "Baseball [is] going along just fine. . . . It's advanced greatly since I was active." According to Cobb, the only exception to baseball's general advancement regarded "the quality of players. We old-timers always think we played great baseball then." Only a few present-day players, such as Stan Musial, came up to Cobb's standards.[24]

As Charles C. Alexander points out in his biography of Cobb, this nostalgic glorification of the past was an active ingredient in Cobb's thought, especially in his later years. In fact, these sentiments probably explain, at least in part, Cobb's stout defense of the reserve clause. In his last few years Cobb would become increasingly pessimistic about the future of the game vis-à-vis other professional sports.[25]

In 1951, however, Cobb was confident that the game could handle its own affairs. Although he was billed for only a brief appearance before the subcommittee, he ended up testifying for an hour and fifteen minutes. The old ballplayer proved to be an entertaining witness who "evoked many chuckles with a homespun account of his early days in baseball."[26] Indeed, as one reads the record of the hearings, it becomes clear that this 1951 baseball inquiry was an enjoyable, refreshing change from the typical issues of domestic and foreign policy for the members of Congress fortunate enough to serve on Celler's subcommittee.

Nevertheless, the sweetness and light that characterized the early hours of the proceedings disappeared when the subcommittee began grilling the president of the National League and soon-to-be commissioner of baseball, Ford Frick.[27] For Frick this was to be the first in a long series of appearances before various congressional subcommittees. In his first, he was questioned on many issues, including the possible expansion of the major leagues to the west coast. Until the Brooklyn Dodgers and New York Giants migrated to Los Angeles and San Francisco, respectively, for the 1958 season, there were no major league franchises located west of St. Louis. This outdated situation was neither a favorable one for organized baseball, nor an acceptable one to Congress. Celler believed that there should come a day "when there will be four major leagues, not two."[28] Frick assured the subcommittee that organized baseball would grow in the near future, either through the graduation of a minor league, such as the Pacific Coast League, or through expansion of the major leagues.[29] Frick's assurances, however, fell on skeptical ears.[30]

Frick was also questioned about the purpose and powers of the commissioner. The subcommittee was particularly interested in this subject because organized baseball was operating without a leader at the time of the investigation. The game's former commissioner, Happy Chandler, had resigned his position on July 15 after numerous skirmishes with owners on a variety of issues. Frick and Warren Giles, president of the Cincinnati Reds, were thought to be the two leading candidates for the job; the major leagues planned to announce Chandler's successor on August 21.

Frick was recalled to testify later in the hearings, after he had been chosen to succeed Chandler. When asked to define the role of the commissioner, Frick responded that the commissioner should represent the players, the public, and the owners, in that order.[31] Again, Frick's reply met with skepticism. Why, the congressmen wondered, could only the owners vote to elect a commissioner? The game's critics felt they had stumbled onto a facet of the national pastime that was neither democratic nor American.

Finally, Frick was asked about the reserve clause. Naturally, he defended baseball's standard contract as nothing more than a long-term agreement, similar to the 30-year deal recently signed by television star Milton Berle. He also relied on the time-worn arguments concerning player distribution and balance of competition that Cobb had used. Frick rounded out his defense of the status quo by reminding the subcommittee that major league teams paid their employees relatively well, and that the game served the fans by providing tickets at such rates as 50 cents for a bleacher seat and one dollar for a spot in the grandstand. Certainly, baseball did not resemble an evil cartel that needed regulating.[32] And on the chance that any cynical subcommittee members remained, Frick warned them that "Baseball is the kid on the sandlot and the shirtsleeve fan in the stands. . . . Like dropping a pebble in a mill pond, any single action taken against any one of the facets of this broad operation is certain to be felt throughout the entire structure."[33]

Happy Chandler was also called to testify before the subcommittee. The congressmen were especially interested in Chandler's testimony because they felt that, inasmuch as he no longer had any official ties to organized baseball, he would be able to give an objective statement to the subcommittee.[34] Chandler's appearance, which lasted over three hours, proved to be a more jovial one than Frick's.[35] The subcommittee members asked the former U.S. senator about his role in the Mexican League episode. In his defense, he stated, "I did not want to punish the boys unless I had to. I think that boys ought to keep their agreements even if it hurts them."[36]

Chandler was generally sympathetic and complimentary, if condescending, toward the players; but as for the owners, he claimed that some of them "don't know where first base is." Yet he was unsure whether the players should be given a voice in the selection of the commissioner, and he was positive that the fans could not have such a role because it would be impractical even if more democratic. Chandler also wanted to use the opportunity before the subcommittee to squelch rumors that he had been the instigator of the congressional investigation. Finally, Chandler, as had all of those before him, defended the reserve clause. He argued that the reserve clause was necessary to prevent "chaos" from ensuing in the national pastime.[37]

Other players and team owners testified in defense of the reserve clause. Fred Hutchinson, American League player representative, stated that the reserve clause was "necessary and reasonable." In an earlier statement to the press, Hutchinson had declared that "the relationship between club owners and players is the best it has been for several years—and they couldn't be any closer in the struggle to uphold the reserve clause." He did believe that the players should have a vote in the selection of the next commissioner, but Hutchinson was otherwise satisfied.[38] Others, including Harold "Pee Wee" Reese, shortstop for the Brooklyn Dodgers, and Lou Boudreau, manager of the Boston Red Sox, firmly defended the reserve clause, although Reese did agree with Hutchinson concerning the players' role in the commissioner selection process.[39]

While the majority of the witnesses supported the status quo, a handful dissented. Chairman Celler recognized that "players may fear to express themselves due to fear of reprisals real or fancied."[40] Among those who bolted from the official line was an unsolicited witness, Father Francis Moore. Moore had played college ball at the University of Santa Clara and semipro ball in the U.S. Army. Moore's basic argument was that the reserve clause was immoral because it *could* strip players of their "God-given ability to play ball," and thus their right to support their families. He further argued that the owners could avoid an imbalance of talent and competition through discipline in purchasing players' contracts.[41] Finally, Moore suggested that public confidence in the game would be higher if the public knew that a player chose to play for a team and was not being forced to do so. And an increased sense of job security among players would lead to less player movement, not more, according to Father Moore.[42]

Danny Gardella was also invited to tell his side of the Mexican League affair, but he failed to appear.[43] His attorney, Fred A. Johnson, did testify before the subcommittee. Johnson generally agreed with Father Moore's opinion of the reserve clause. He opposed the reserve clause on the ground that it represented a clear violation of free trade and free labor. Johnson suggested a compromise system (similar to the one the National Football League would adopt in 1993), whereby a team could reserve a select few of its top players.[44]

The subcommittee listened to testimony from one other dissenter, a former minor leaguer named Ross Horning. Somewhat of a "surprise witness" because he was not on the scheduled list of witnesses, Horning, a graduate student at George Washington University, had played as an infielder for several minor league clubs, including the Sioux Falls club in the Northern League. He testified against the reserve clause, claiming it made things especially bad for no-name minor leaguers, if not for superstars like Ted Williams. Horning failed to offer any practical reforms for the status quo, but did suggest that players' contracts needed to be more binding on both sides.[45]

Undoubtedly, many would-be stars trapped in the minors concurred with Horning's statement. Chairman Celler, for example, received a bitter letter from the wife of a minor league pitcher who was upset because the subcommittee did not call more minor leaguers to testify. She asked, "Ty Cobb, Branch Rickey—what do they know of the average ballplayer?" Interestingly, the woman wrote Celler the next day and pleaded with the chairman to destroy her previous letter. She feared that her husband would be embarrassed by her complaints and possibly divorce her as a result.[46]

Yet such rebels were scarce, or at least quiet, both in and out of the hearing room. Certainly the subcommittee, and Chairman Celler particularly, could have worked harder to seek out the disgruntled in organized baseball. But for all of their complaints, Ross Horning and others like him could never draw a crowd to a hearing room, as could Ty Cobb or Pee Wee Reese.

A final testimony worth looking at is that of Philip K. Wrigley, president of the Chicago Cubs. Although Wrigley defended the reserve clause, he also felt that baseball should be placed under the antitrust laws. He advocated a limited exemption for the reserve clause but not the "blank check" variety contained in the three pending bills, because he recognized that in many ways professional baseball was a business like any other. Wrigley's suggested course proved to be the one many legislators would pursue in the late 1950s and early 1960s. On the whole, Wrigley viewed the hearings as a positive thing, even if no legislation were to result. To the Chicago Cubs president, the investigation was a "cataclysmic" event which would force the owners to ban together and the game to evolve to a higher level.[47]

Not everyone shared Wrigley's enthusiasm for the hearings as they drew to a close, however. Representative Kenneth B. Keating of New York, ranking Republican on the subcommittee, never did "warm up to the hearings with the state of the world as it is."[48] He later warned, "Congress better be darned careful before it starts tampering with baseball. . . . At a time when the world is on fire, it seems to me that we have more important things to do." Keating also believed that the public was unhappy with Congress: "I think if we were umpires, we would now be dodging pop bottles."[49] The *Sporting News* agreed that the average fan was "bewildered by the investigation. . . [and] baffled by what he thinks is a move by Congress to realign the major leagues." One fan declared "baseball is the cleanest sport we've got. If congressmen haven't got anything better to do, why don't they look into boxing?"[50] As for Chairman Celler, editorialized the *New York Daily News*, "We think Mr. Celler would do well to bench himself for a while and then go meddle with some other business. . . . Manny's efforts to disrupt the national sport are not appreciated by anybody we know of."[51]

Chairman Celler promised that the subcommittee would not attempt a "hurried solution" to the "complex" problems within organized baseball.[52] Indeed, the subcommittee had moved slowly and deliberately with the national pastime. Late into October, after sixteen days of hearings and several thousand pages of testimony, the subcommittee retired to draft and approve a report of its proceedings. It produced a 200-page report that was full of interesting information about organized baseball, but that advised no action be taken regarding the national pastime.

The report concluded with the five options that were open to the subcommittee: 1) to outlaw the reserve clause by placing organized baseball completely under the antitrust laws; 2) to do the opposite— that is, grant unlimited exemption for organized baseball; 3) to create a national baseball code, enforceable by a special federal agency; 4) to grant limited exemption for the reserve clause; or 5) to do nothing. The subcommittee recommended option 5, declaring that it would be premature to act before the courts decided on the matter.[53] (There were several court cases pending at the time of the investigation.) Thus began what Lee Lowenfish and Tony Lupien have termed a "jurisdictional volleyball" game between the legislative and judicial branches of the federal government.[54]

There are some interesting and important observations that should be made concerning this first post-World War II investigation into professional sports. In *The Governmental Process*, David B. Truman outlines three functions of congressional committee hearings. First, they provide an opportunity for the interest groups involved to provide information to the committee or subcommittee. Second, hearings serve as a propaganda channel through which the interest groups involved may present their positions to the public. "At some points in the development of a measure, in fact, the primary purpose of hearings lies in their propaganda value."[55] Thus, inasmuch as the group that is being investigated is keenly interested in how it is being perceived by the public through the hearings, it tends to send well-known, colorful witnesses to testify, particularly if the bill under debate has a strong chance of being passed. Third, the public hearing serves as a type of safety valve relieving differences and conflicts within interest groups.[56]

The 1951 baseball hearings and the numerous hearings and investigations into professional sports that followed fulfilled the functions listed above, particularly the first two. Indeed, the 200-page report is packed with interesting, important data concerning the baseball and has served as a valuable reference source not only to Congress but to scholars of the game. The 1951 hearings, as well as its many successors, certainly served the purposes of information gathering and education.

Moreover, the hearings clearly worked as a propaganda channel for organized baseball. The statements of Ford Frick, for example, were as much propaganda as anything else. Yet such propaganda was, and is, common to congressional hearings and investigations in general. Indeed, as William L. Morrow has pointed out, congressional hearings are not solely information gathering events; for if they were, interest groups would send only technical advisors and not more popular, if less knowledgeable, figures to speak in behalf of the group's interests.[57] In the case of organized baseball, this would mean sending more lawyers and fewer outfielders and shortstops.

As mentioned earlier, however, lawyers and other colorless witnesses simply cannot fill a hearing room or bring as much public pressure to bear on an issue as can an outfielder or shortstop. Although all of the professional sports used this tactic at one time or another (including professional boxing in the pre-World War II era), organized baseball made an art of it in the 1950s when its public image was at its strongest.

Of course, the hearing room is not only a stage for the interest group or industry being investigated but one for the committee members as well. They are at least equally concerned with attracting a large amount of positive public attention. Observing the numerous motives a particular congressman might have for attracting public attention to a hearing, Ralph Huitt has noted, "He may wish to make himself a national leader, build a reputation as a subject matter expert, advertise himself to the constituency, do a favor for a supporter, discharge some of his own aggression—the list could be a long one."[58] Senator Estes Kefauver of Tennessee wrote bitingly, "Congress has its share of crackpots, cheap publicity-seekers, shirkers, and chiselers."[59] Concerning the congressional investigation, Senator Sam Ervin of North Carolina observed, it "can be the catalyst that spurs Congress and the public to support vital reforms in our nation's laws. Or it can debase our principles, invade the privacy of our citizens, and afford a platform for demagogues and the rankest partisans."[60]

This is not to suggest that Emanuel Celler was either a "cheap publicity-seeker" or one of the "rankest partisans" of his day (though this was undoubtedly debatable among some of his contemporaries); indeed, the publicity surrounding the 1951 hearings tended to be more negative than positive. But it is to point out that hearings and investigations provide nice opportunities for publicity and media attention.[61]

Indeed, the fact that more Ross Hornings were not called to testify in the 1950s is the responsibility of both Congress and organized baseball. More unknown minor leaguers could have been either called by the subcommittee or sent as spokesmen by organized baseball, but both parties had a strong interest in hearing the game's stars speak publicly. Too, subcommittee members simply had more fun questioning Ty Cobb and Pee Wee Reese than Ross Horning. Many of these congressmen and their successors were, like so many other Americans, fans of the game. Babe Ruth was no longer around to testify, but Ty Cobb was. In sum, from a fan's perspective, it is not too difficult to understand why congressmen consistently preferred to speak with a professional sport's stars rather than its lesser-known figures; indeed, it is understandable, if not entirely noble.

Moreover, the results of the 1951 baseball hearings were typical of later hearings on professional sports and congressional committee hearings in general. The fact that the bills never made it out of the subcommittee in which they were debated was not unusual. In this Congress, the 82nd, 8,568 bills were introduced in the House, 1,456 of those were reported, and 1,340 were passed.[62] Such statistics not only held for the House and Senate in later congresses, but the disparity between bills introduced and bills passed actually increased. Of course, the number of bills enacted was still fewer. Out of the 12,062 bills introduced into the House and Senate in the 82nd Congress, 1,617 were enacted.[63]

In other words, bridging the gap between committee and floor is a long, complicated process in both houses of Congress, though a slightly easier one in the Senate, and the large majority of bills that are debated in subcommittee rooms never see the light of day. Woodrow Wilson observed, "as a rule, a bill committed is a bill doomed. When it goes from a clerk's desk to a committee room it crosses a parliamentary bridge of sighs to dim dungeons of silence whence it will never return. The means and times of its deaths are unknown, but its friends never see it again."[64] Congress always has and always will spend time and tax dollars debating issues and bills that never come close to becoming law—such is the nature of our political system. Thus, while it is easy to become frustrated with

Congress's legislative inactivity concerning professional sports, especially in light of the numerous hearings and investigations on the subject, one must keep in mind that this behavior is typical in the life of the national legislature. In this sense, the 1951 baseball investigation was less than extraordinary.

Nevertheless, most contemporaries seemed satisfied with the report and results of the hearings. Representative Keating applauded the report, but still claimed that the investigation was too premature to be useful and that the public money spent on it could have been put to better use. Commissioner Frick assured Congress that organized baseball had gained a "keen awareness" of its problems, but he added that he did not think "baseball people will agree 100 per cent with the findings of the committee."[65] On the whole, however, organized baseball was pleased with the legislative inaction of Congress, and Commissioner Frick congratulated Chairman Celler and his subcommittee for "a job well done."[66] Arthur Daley, sports columnist for the *New York Times*, also commended the subcommittee's inaction: "It's truly wonderful in this day and age when anyone, particularly a legislator, decides to mind his own business."[67] Everyone was not pleased; Chairman Celler also received a letter from "a busted minor leaguer" requesting Congress to place statutory limits on the reserve clause, if it could not be totally eliminated.[68] The liberal weekly magazine *Nation* acidly agreed: "Statements of living immortals notwithstanding, Congress should recognize major-league baseball as the major industry it is and outlaw the reserve clause as an improper restraint of trade."[69]

As for organized baseball, it effectively maintained an image in the hearts and minds of Americans as the pastoral, innocent, and noble national pastime. Professional baseball in 1951 was everything that professional boxing was not and everything that professional football and basketball wanted to become. While it is true that organized baseball failed to persuade Congress to pass the legislative antitrust exemption it desired, the game was successful in convincing the subcommittee to maintain the status quo. And for organized baseball, maintenance of the status quo meant continued antitrust exemption. Thus, beyond a general education of Congress and some members of the public, the only result of the 1951 hearings was the need for more of the same. After all, what congressman would be bold enough in the early 1950s to risk the chance of negatively affecting the "American game" played in an "American fashion?"

Chapter 3

Stengelese, the Mahatma, and the Baseball-Badgering Bill, 1957–60

Although organized baseball emerged from its first meeting with Congress unscathed, the future of the reserve clause was still very uncertain. One source reported that the "dominant feeling" was that the Supreme Court would, if given the chance, strike down the reserve clause as an unreasonable restraint of trade or as a violation of the prohibition in the Thirteenth Amendment to the Constitution against involuntary servitude.[1] In 1953, in fact, the high court got another chance to remove organized baseball's historic antitrust exemption in the *Toolson* case. The case involved a New York Yankees player who sued his club because it blacklisted him after he failed to report to a Yankees farm team.[2] On November 9, 1953, the Supreme Court affirmed baseball's exempt status under the antitrust laws on the grounds that it was a matter for the national legislature to settle and, inasmuch as Congress failed to take away baseball's exemption in 1951, the Court did not feel it could do so in 1953.[3]

Although organized baseball had survived its closest call in the courts, other professional sports were not so lucky. In 1955, in the case of *International Boxing Club v. U.S.,* the Supreme Court ruled that professional boxing was a business that belonged under the antitrust laws.[4] Then in 1957 the high court placed professional football under the antitrust laws with its decision in the case of *Radovich v. National Football League.* The Court admitted that its ruling was "unrealistic, inconsistent, [and] illogical" in light of its ruling in the *Toolson* case. Yet the opinion also stated that the "orderly way to eliminate error or discrimination . . . is by legislation and not by court action." Congress could be more "accommodative" because public hearings would "be more likely to protect the industry and the public alike."[5] Thus, by the end of February 1957 the major professional sports were inconsistently arranged in relation to the antitrust laws. Moreover, their positions were especially precarious

29

because they had been gained at the hands of the courts rather than the hands of Congress.

Representative Celler's subcommittee on monopoly power, which he still chaired in 1957, seized the opportunity afforded by these Supreme Court decisions to open another round of legislative hearings on the subject of professional sports. The subcommittee heard arguments on a handful of bills that fell into one of three categories: 1) to subject all professional sports, including baseball, to the antitrust laws; 2) to subject all professional sports to the antitrust laws, but with exemptions for certain practices relating to league balance, such as the reserve clause; or 3) to grant all professional sports complete antitrust exemption.[6]

Chairman Celler's own bill, H.R. 10378, was the measure most hotly debated by the subcommittee and its witnesses. The Celler bill fell into the first of the three categories noted above. If enacted, the bill would have placed all aspects and practices of professional sports under the antitrust laws *except* those practices that the courts deemed a "reasonably necessary" restraint of trade.[7] Thus, practices related to the equalization of player strength, franchise territorial rights, the telecasting and broadcasting of games, and the preservation of public confidence in the honesty of sports contests would have to undergo the "reasonably necessary" test in the courts to determine their worthiness for antitrust exemption.

Celler's attitude toward baseball had become more hostile since the 1951 hearings. He called the reserve clause "barbarous" and added, "If we do away with the reserve clause, baseball would attract more young players who don't like to be chattel slaves." Much of Celler's increased hostility toward the game was caused by rumors that Walter O'Malley, owner of the Brooklyn Dodgers, was considering moving the team to the west coast. These rumors would surface regularly throughout the hearings.

Beyond the Supreme Court decisions and Celler's fear of a possible move by the Dodgers, the hearings were called because of the efforts of Bert Bell, commissioner of the National Football League.[8] Following the *Radovich* case, Bell and the NFL lobbied Congress to give football the antitrust exemption enjoyed by baseball.

Thus, the House held fifteen days of subcommittee hearings on the antitrust laws and professional sports. Four of the six subcommittee members, including ranking Republican Kenneth B.

Keating, had been involved in the 1951 hearings. Keating himself sponsored a moderate bill aimed at placing all professional sports under the antitrust laws, but allowing automatic exemptions for certain aspects, such as the reserve clause, so that they would not have to survive the "reasonably necessary" test in court. He argued that such a "mixture of sport and business" required "special treatment." Keating further criticized the Celler bill because, he felt, it left the tough questions up to the courts. "It takes no courage to engage in this kind of buck-passing," he declared.[9]

Although the hearings concerned all professional sports, the subcommittee paid most attention to organized baseball. The game was represented once again by Ford Frick. The commissioner seemed more confident and assured in 1957 than in 1951, as he told the subcommittee that the best solution was legislation granting all professional sports complete immunity from the antitrust laws. Frick testified that he had grave concerns about the Celler bill, which would, he feared, lead to "burdensome and protracted litigation." As Frick saw matters, the "reserve clause and territorial rights" were the "keystones of the game"; to outlaw them would "result in the abolition of the professional game as we now know it."[10]

The subcommittee also heard testimony from Walter O'Malley. Chairman Celler grilled O'Malley about the swirling rumors of a potential franchise move for the 1958 season. Although he questioned O'Malley for more than two hours, Celler failed to receive a definite answer concerning the Dodgers' plans. O'Malley, an attorney by trade, was polite and congenial, but evasive. And although Representative Keating believed that the residents of Brooklyn still had reason for hope, Chairman Celler concluded from his discussion with O'Malley that the issue was "all cut and dried." The *Sporting News* agreed with Celler, reporting that only a "last-ditch move by civic authorities . . . will keep the Bums in Brooklyn."[11] Indeed, O'Malley's testimony confirmed Celler's fears and toughened his resolve to bring baseball under the antitrust laws.

A handful of players testified as well. The players were less unified concerning the reserve clause in 1957 than they had been six years earlier. One former big-league star blasted away at organized baseball. Bob Feller compared the reserve system to "peonage" and described the owners as "arrogant" men who treated their players "like children" and regarded them as "pawns." Feller concluded that if the owners' attitudes did not change, they would be more harmful to the game than complete application of the antitrust laws.[12] American League President Will Harridge was "shocked and surprised" by Feller's testimony, while National League President Warren Giles called it "unfair."[13]

An interesting sidelight to the 1957 hearings was the controversy that followed Bob Feller's testimony. Feller was to appear at Wrigley Field in Los Angeles for "Bob Feller Night," a major-league sponsored baseball clinic for youngsters. Without any explanation, the clinic was canceled. Naturally, the owners were accused of using intimidation tactics on Feller because of his hostile testimony. Republican Representative Patrick J. Hillings of California led the charge against the owners. He advocated recalling all of the players to have them testify under oath. Chairman Celler quickly snuffed out this proposal, and, after Commissioner Frick promised to look into the affair, the episode died.[14] (Lee Lowenfish and Tony Lupien have suggested that intimidation tactics by the owners toward the players were common during this period.)[15]

Other players and ex-players seemed to feel that Feller had gone too far. Most of them, including Stan Musial, firmly defended the reserve clause and the status quo generally.[16] Joe Garagiola, another ex-player and now a St. Louis Cardinals announcer, wrote to Representative Keating that he was disturbed by Feller's testimony. Garagiola, who characterized himself as a far more "average" player than Feller, wrote that he had never felt like a peon or knew anyone else who did.[17]

Aside from the numerous representatives of organized baseball, the subcommittee heard testimony from Bert Bell of the National Football League and Clarence Campbell of the National Hockey League. Bell testified that the NFL was seeking "legislative relief" from the courts because the *Radovich* decision and others that might come in the future could have disastrous effects on professional football.[18] As for the NHL, Clarence Campbell stated that professional hockey supported the Keating bill over the Celler bill. Campbell concluded, however, that the best thing for professional sports would be for Congress to grant them complete exemption.[19] Following these witnesses, the hearings drew to a close early in August.

Although it took nearly a year, on June 24, 1958, the Celler bill eventually reached the floor of the House. A debate quickly ensued between supporters of that bill and Keating's. The two bills were nearly identical, but they differed significantly in that Celler's version would force monopolistic practices to pass the "reasonably necessary" test in the courts and Keating's version would grant such practices complete antitrust immunity. Eventually, Keating's forces rammed an amendment through the floor that struck the words "reasonably necessary" from the Celler bill. Soon after, the House passed Keating's version of H.R. 10378 by an "overwhelming" voice vote.[20]

A confident Keating had predicted that the bill would pass and would represent "a grandslam homer, a touchdown, an overtime victory, and a hat-trick rolled into one."[21] The bill certainly represented all of that to the officialdom of professional sports. Ford Frick and Clarence Campbell lobbied Keating to defeat the Celler bill and push his own version.[22] Yet for all the confidence of Frick, Campbell, and Keating, H.R. 10378 was a long way from becoming public law.

Although the Keating bill had slipped through the House, everyone involved knew that time was running out in the 85th Congress, and that the bill would face a much stiffer challenge in the Senate. Estes Kefauver, Democratic chairman of the Senate Subcommittee on Anti-Trust and Monopoly, hurriedly scheduled hearings for the second week of July. Kefauver made it clear from the outset that he was uncomfortable with the Keating bill because he thought it offered too broad an exemption for professional sports.[23] Like Celler, Kefauver had a national reputation as a leading trustbuster in Congress, and despite having been a three-sport athlete in high school and a solid football player for the University of Tennessee, he was less than generous to the various professional sports leagues.[24] However, unlike Celler, Kefauver was not the chairman of the Senate's Judiciary Committee; thus, his power and influence were more limited than his counterpart's in the House.

The hearings were scheduled to begin on July 9, the day after the baseball All-Star game, which was played that summer in Baltimore. The Senate subcommittee "assured itself of a full house" by inviting a handful of the All-Stars, including Ted Williams, Mickey Mantle, and Stan Musial, to testify in Washington the day after the game. The subcommittee also invited Yankee manager Casey Stengel and Albert B. Chandler, who now served as the governor of Kentucky.[25] The measure in question was S. 4070, a bill introduced by Senator Thomas C. Hennings of Missouri and identical to the Keating bill passed in the House the previous June.[26]

One of the first witnesses was none other than Representative Celler. Celler stated that Congress had been "waylaid" the previous June by the professional sports "lobbies." He also lashed out at the owners, who, he said, "wish to be like feudal barons—and treat the public as serfs." As for the players, Celler believed that the discontented ones had been coerced into line and that the "contented baseball players . . . have had their tongues loosened" by money to support the status quo.[27]

Regardless of what Celler thought of them, the All-Stars who testified on July 9 did appear to be content with things as they were. But before any of the players sat down in the witness chair, the hearing room was treated to the amusing testimony of Casey Stengel. The Yankees' manager and the All-Stars had lured television cameras, still cameramen, and a standing-room-only crowd of more than 300 into the Senate caucus room. Stengel appeared before the subcommittee "impeccably dressed in a grey suit, white shirt and dark tie."[28] As youngsters approached the All-Stars seated behind Stengel for their autographs, the "Ol' Perfessor" began his testimony. Although he never clearly supported any of the proposed bills, Stengel—speaking in the unique fashion that sportswriters had dubbed "Stengelese"—strongly supported the national pastime. "Baseball," he declared, "has been run cleaner than any business that was ever put out in the 100 years at the present time. It is the most honest profession I think that we have." When asked by Kefauver why baseball wanted S. 4070, Stengel replied, "I would say I would not know but I would say the reason why they would want it passed is to keep baseball going as the highest paid ball that has gone into baseball and from the baseball angle, I am not going to speak of any other sport."[29]

The testimony represented Stengelese in its highest form. One headline read, "Stengel Positive in His Views—But What Did He Say?" Another report stated that Stengel left the subcommittee "bewildered and baffled," and that "Ol' Casey proved you don't have to take the Fifth Amendment to evade a Senatorial question."[30] His biographer has suggested that "the Stengel legend peaked on July 9, 1958." But he adds that Stengel's testimony was more than a mere snow job to avoid the tough questions posed by the senators. Stengel did not believe that the owners had earned the trust necessary to grant the game complete antitrust exemption, but he also had some resentment toward the players for failing to include managers and others in their pension plan; thus, Stengel felt sincere ambivalence concerning the antitrust issue.

Nonetheless, Stengel's appearance proved the most humorous and publicized in the history of congressional hearings on professional sports. The Ol' Perfessor brought the crowd and subcommittee to laughter on a number of occasions, and one senator said afterward, with tears in his eyes from laughter, that Stengel's statement was "the best entertainment we have had around here for a long time."[31]

Stengel was followed by a panel of All-Stars, including Mantle, Williams, and Musial. Mantle spoke first and brought the house down one more time by simply stating, "My views are just about the same as Casey's." Kefauver responded, "If you could define what Casey's views were, it would be a service to this committee."[32] When the laughter died down, the All-Stars one by one defended the reserve clause and the status quo in general. Ted Williams, casually dressed in a tieless sports shirt and coat, stated, "I have been playing baseball for 22 years, and I can't remember, especially since I have been playing with the Red Sox, of any one case that there has been a gripe about a salary over the years."[33]

Like Williams, Musial showed great faith in the owners' ability to lead baseball and also claimed that he had never been dissatisfied with his salary or the St. Louis Cardinals organization to which he was reserved.[34] One reporter cynically wrote that the exchange was "a standoff. . . . The Senators don't know a thing about baseball and the players don't know a thing about law."[35] Yet July 9 was a standoff that greatly benefited baseball, inasmuch its biggest stars had upheld the status quo during a widely reported public hearing.

As the hearings moved through July, however, organized baseball began to take considerable criticism. Several ex-players gave the game something less than a glowing recommendation. Although he had tempered his views somewhat, Bob Feller was still dissatisfied with the status quo. He did concede that the reserve clause was the "necessary backbone of baseball," but he suggested that salary arbitration should become available for players who failed to reach an agreement with their team's owners. Feller also stated that, while he supported the Keating bill, he felt that the players ought to have a voice in the commissioner selection process.[36]

Jackie Robinson was another ex-player who held reform-minded ideas. Like Feller, Robinson believed that the reserve clause was necessary in some form, but he suggested that it be limited to five or six years. (Ty Cobb had suggested such a plan early in his career, but it would be the mid-1970s before arbitration and free-agency would dramatically change the face of organized baseball.) Finally, Robinson agreed with Feller that the players should have a greater say in the selection of the commissioner.[37] Except for Feller and Robinson, however, the witnesses from organized baseball supported the status quo.

Representatives from professional football were also given a relatively small amount of time before the subcommittee. Bert Bell testified that the National Football League strongly supported the Keating bill because the "reasonably necessary" language of the Celler bill would lead to expensive litigation.[38] But he agreed with the testimony of William Howerton, player for the Green Bay Packers and president of the National Football League Players Association, who testified that the Keating bill would seriously jeopardize the position of the players by stripping them of whatever leverage they had in court.[39] Professional football, having more to gain and less to lose in Congress as a result of the *Radovich* case, was accommodative to any congressional effort to legislate a clear position for professional sports under the antitrust laws.

Such legislative relief was not to come from the 85th Congress. During the first week of August, Kefauver's subcommittee voted four to two in favor of tabling the Keating bill. Kefauver discussed the committee's action in a letter to United Press International, explaining that the members of the subcommittee, including himself, believed that the Keating bill offered too broad an exemption to professional sports.[40] Thus, as expected, the Keating bill died in the Senate subcommittee; everyone involved in the antitrust and professional sports issue would have to start from scratch in the 86th Congress.

Starting from scratch did not bother the trustbuster from Tennessee, however. Senator Kefauver moved quickly in 1959 to introduce a bill containing his solution to the problem of antitrust and organized baseball. Kefauver's bill would change shape a number of times throughout the 86th Congress, but in its basic form the Kefauver bill was identical to the Celler bill, although it contained a number of novel provisions, such as one that would limit the number of players a particular team could reserve at one time. Kefauver attempted to get Keating, recently elected to the U.S. Senate, to co-sponsor his bill. Senator Keating would have no part of it, but rather reintroduced his House-passed sports bill in the Senate.[41] Chairman Kefauver scheduled another round of legislative hearings for July 28-32 to debate the merits of the Kefauver and Keating bills.

The day before the hearings began, a press conference was called in New York by William A. Shea to announce the formation of the Continental League, a proposed third major league. The mayor of New York had appointed Shea to head a committee for the purpose of securing a second major league team for the city. With Congress pressuring the major leagues for expansion, a third league seemed like a good way to get a second team in the Big Apple. As of July 27, the Continental League had financial backers in Toronto, Houston, Minneapolis, Denver, and New York. Shea planned to have a third circuit comprised of eight to twelve teams that would begin play in the 1961 season. Finally, the Continental League would appoint the 78-year old Branch Rickey as its first commissioner. Shea stated that the third league hoped to make an arrangement with the existing major leagues, but if it failed to do so during a meeting scheduled for August 18, the new league would seek congressional assistance and inaugurate play without the help of the majors.[42]

As the hearings convened on the heels of Shea's press conference, the purpose behind the Kefauver bill became clear. Claiming that some major league teams controlled up to 450 players, Kefauver was trying to free up some talent for the Continental League. In its original form, the Kefauver bill placed an 80-player limit on major league teams. Such a limit would allow a franchise to control all of its major leaguers plus one minor league team. The Kefauver bill also defined a team's territory as the area within a 35-mile radius of the ballpark. This definition was much narrower than the one in use by the major leagues.[43] Kefauver made it clear that his goal was to facilitate a third major league, although the provisions of his bill, particularly the two mentioned above, were bitterly opposed by organized baseball and its supporters. Senator Keating called the Kefauver bill a "baseball badgering bill."[44] Comparing his bill to Kefauver's, Keating said, "One road leads to stringent and unwarranted control by the Federal Government. . . . The other road leads to a continuation of practices which have been tried and found acceptable."[45]

Thus, when the witnesses began appearing before the subcommittee, the battle lines had been clearly drawn. Ford Frick was called upon to offer organized baseball's opinion of the two bills. Of course, Frick vehemently opposed the Kefauver bill, especially the provision placing an 80-player limit on major league franchises. He explained to the subcommittee that it took more than 30 minor leaguers to produce one bona-fide major league player. Thus, Frick predicted that the bill would "wreck both the major and minor leagues and . . . lower the quality of professional baseball play." As for the Continental League, Frick warned, "I don't know of anything that will slow up a third league more than being limited to eighty players." Rather, he suggested that the quickest way for a third league to get off the ground would be for it to adopt standard major league practices.[46]

Branch Rickey testified on behalf of the proposed Continental League. Like Casey Stengel's the previous year, Rickey's testimony was entertaining and highly publicized. The *Sporting News* reported that "the Mahatma [as he was called in the New York press] was a symphony in brown—his butterfly bow tie, summer-weight suit, oxfords, horned-rimmed glasses and unlit cigar. There was no need to tell the movie and TV cameramen that this was Branch Rickey, baseball's elder statesman, posturing." Indeed, Rickey carried a cane as well, which he periodically rapped on the witness table in order to punctuate his testimony.[47]

During his brief statement, Rickey agreed with Frick's analysis that a player limit would do more harm than good for the infant Continental League. He assured the subcommittee and the major leagues that he did not want to see damage done to the minor leagues, and that he felt the reserve clause was "essential" to the health of professional baseball. He did suggest, however, that an unrestricted draft of players on major league rosters might be the best formula for getting the Continental League off the ground.[48] Rickey's testimony was as much show as anything else, as no representative from the Continental League wanted to risk torpedoing the meeting planned for August 18 between the Continental League and the major leagues.

Witnesses from other professional sports were also called upon to discuss another provision of the Kefauver bill. If enacted, the Kefauver bill would have directly influenced professional football and basketball by allowing a college draftee to refuse to play for the team that selected him and accept offers from other teams in the league. Kefauver, of course, wanted college graduates to have some say in their future, but the idea was anathema to the National Football

League. Bert Bell asked Kefauver why any player would be willing to consent to the draft if he could opt to play for another team in order to make more money or live close to family. He reminded the subcommittee that in the last thirteen years, eight different teams had won the NFL championship. Bell was convinced that the Kefauver bill would lead to "intricate problems" and damage the competitive player strength in professional football.[49] Maurice Podoloff, president of the National Basketball League, generally agreed with Bell and warned that the Kefauver bill, if passed, would "ultimately destroy professional basketball."[50] Both men supported the Keating bill wholeheartedly.

But the primary issue of the hearings was the proposed Continental League and organized baseball's reaction to it. Inasmuch as the two sides were scheduled to meet on August 18, the 1959 congressional hearings and the Kefauver Bill were a few weeks premature. As the August 18 meeting approached, representatives of the Continental League appeared confident. William Shea believed that a round-robin-type World Series would be played within two years. But Shea quickly added that if the majors failed to accommodate the Continental League, it would seek legislative help from Congress.[51]

Organized baseball, though, seemed willing to cooperate as the meeting date approached. Frick stated that he believed a third major league was inevitable and seemed willing to give the Continental League a fair shake.[52] Others in organized baseball were more closed-minded, however. Larry MacPhail, retired president of the Yankees, argued that a third league would have little chance of survival, and that a safer route would be for the existing major leagues to expand from ten to twelve teams each.[53] The Continental League hoped that MacPhail represented the minority view and urged the subcommittee to take a wait-and-see attitude concerning the Kefauver bill. Kefauver concurred with the wishes of the Continental League, but warned that the subcommittee was "very interested in every action taken in regard to the Continental League. . . . You might say baseball is under surveillance, even under a shotgun."[54] Thus, the subcommittee voted four to two in favor of shelving the Kefauver bill until organized baseball and the Continental League had a chance to come to terms.

Ultimately, the two sides were unable to come to terms during the late summer and fall of 1959. The primary sticking point was the indemnity to be paid to the minor league clubs whose territory would be invaded by the new Continental teams. The fact was, however, that major league owners were simply less enthusiastic about a third major league than they were about expanding the two existing leagues. William Shea, as he promised, lobbied Congress for legislative assistance. But it did not take much coaxing to get Senator Kefauver to reintroduce his bill in 1960.

The 1960 version of the Kefauver bill was slightly different from the previous year's version. The latest bill was divided into two titles. Title I exempted professional football, basketball, and hockey from the antitrust laws in much the same way as the old Keating bill had done. Title II, however, applied to baseball only and provided for a 100-player limit, with 60 of those vulnerable to an annual unrestricted draft. Also, the narrow definition of a team's territory contained in the earlier Kefauver bill remained in the later version. The clear purpose of Title II was to encourage major league expansion.

Hearings on the updated Kefauver bill were held on May 19-20, 1960, but before the hearings got under way, the major protagonists made their opinions known. William Shea proclaimed the Continental League "one hundred per cent behind the bill. It is our only hope of getting players and going into business." Although Ford Frick claimed that he was neither a promoter of the Continental League nor a hatchet man for the majors, he called the bill "preposterous" and "vicious." Warren Giles warned that "it will ultimately do great harm to a great game," and George Weiss, general manager of the Yankees, added, "I cannot believe Congress will take it seriously."[55]

The subcommittee first heard from representatives of the Continental League. The man still leading the charge for the proposed major league was Branch Rickey. Rickey told the congressmen that although he had been more ambivalent about the Kefauver bill the previous summer, his enthusiasm for the bill had grown as a result of blatant foot-dragging by major league owners. Rickey claimed that the major leagues had not dealt with the Continental Leaguers in good faith, and that the time had come for congressional action. He reported to the subcommittee that the Continental League had filled out its eight-team circuit, which now consisted of teams in New York, Toronto, Atlanta, Minneapolis-St. Paul, Dallas, Denver, Houston, and Buffalo.[56] Rickey also persuaded the subcommittee that the Kefauver bill would save the existing majors, inasmuch as it would help put an end to the practice of bonus signings, a practice that was costing major league teams a great deal of money.

Moreover, Rickey claimed, organized baseball was the only business in America that had not changed in more than 50 years. The game had forgotten its priorities, which, according to Rickey, were "the public . . . first, the player . . . second . . . [and] the club owner . . . third."[57] The Mahatma then resorted to patriotism by telling the subcommittee that "the sport is known throughout the world as the great national game of the United States. . . . [It makes] Americans everywhere forget the last syllable of a man's name or the pigmentation of his skin."[58] Thus, nationalism and the melting pot were used again to describe baseball in a congressional hearing, but this time for the purpose of *challenging* the status quo. Rickey pledged to "extend myself to my death" to save the Continental League. Afterward he urged Senator Philip Hart of Michigan to work for the passage of the Kefauver bill "or a bill more liberal."[59]

Representing the existing major leagues, Commissioner Frick stoutly opposed the Kefauver bill throughout his testimony. The commissioner's central argument was that the bill, by limiting the number of players a major league team could control, would ultimately destroy what remained of the minor leagues.[60] He told the subcommittee that the bill would destroy existing working agreements between major and minor league teams, and in the process eliminate major-league support for more than 80 minor league clubs. Frick warned that if the bill passed, the majors would be able to service only six minor leagues.[61]

Many observers felt that the commissioner had lost his credibility concerning the minors, as the number of minor league teams had dropped dramatically during his tenure. Referring to Frick, one ex-congressman said, "Personally, I don't pay much attention to a doctor whose patients are all in the cemetery."[62] Undaunted, Frick concluded his testimony by pointing to the game's nearly 100 years of "honorable self-regulation," and by pleading with the sub-committee either to approve the Keating bill or strike Title II from the Kefauver bill and include organized baseball under Title I.[63]

Following the brief hearings, the Kefauver bill was placed on the Senate calendar for June 13. It went to the floor without recom-mendation from the subcommittee, because of deep divisions within that body. The subcommittee members and the representatives from the Continental League and the major leagues lobbied hard for their sides throughout the first three weeks of June. Organized baseball blitzed congressmen, particularly the subcommittee members, with letters predicting the destruction of the minors and pleading with the recipients to work to eliminate Title II and include baseball under Title I.[64]

Branch Rickey and William Shea also lobbied Congress vigorously on behalf of their Continental League, as did fans who favored the proposed league. One wrote to Senator Keating, "I am just a baseball fan without a team to follow in the biggest city in the country. (Like a lot of fans here, I don't care for the Yankees.)" He went on to warn Keating that if he did not stop his "hypocritical" behavior and support the Kefauver bill, the fans would "repay" him "some day *pretty good*, believe me."[65]

Asked about the chances his bill had on the floor, Senator Kefauver responded, "Darned if I know." In fact, Kefauver did not fight hard for the bill because his attention was consumed by hearings on the drug industry and by the difficult reelection campaign facing him in the fall.[66] Senator Hart, however, devoted a lot of time to the bill. He opposed the bill and stated that in this case Congress should remain "in the grandstands."[67] Hart's efforts paid off. When the Kefauver bill reached the floor of the Senate on June 28, it was easily sent back to committee by a vote of 73 to 12.[68] A relieved Commissioner Frick said, "It was a bad piece of legislation" that would have hurt everybody. He promptly wrote Senator Hart to congratulate him on the "magnificent job" he had done on getting the Kefauver bill defeated on the Senate floor.[69] William Shea described the setback as "a severe blow," but he added, "we are not finished."[70]

Actually, the defeat of the Kefauver bill did finish the Continental League. Although the major leagues promised to give the Continental League until December to pay indemnities to the minor league teams whose territory they would invade, the majors also announced in July that they had plans to expand each league by at least two teams for the 1962 season. The planners of the third league did not wait until December, but gave the majors a green light to proceed with their expansion plans.[71] As promised, in 1961 the American League added franchises in Los Angeles and Minneapolis-St. Paul, and in 1962 the National League picked up teams in Houston and New York. Branch Rickey and William Shea were generally pleased with the outcome of the whole affair; after all, three of the four new major league franchises had been part of the planned Continental League. Observers accurately credited both Rickey and Senator Kefauver for the expansion within the two major leagues.[72]

Indeed, although the Continental League and the Kefauver bill failed to reach fruition, they did achieve their ultimate goal—expansion of major league baseball.

Chapter 4

Going on for Decades, 1964–92

Although Senator Estes Kefauver had promised to continue his efforts to have organized baseball placed under the antitrust laws, he was unable to do so before he died of a heart ailment in August 1963.[1] Kefauver had served as the chairman of the Senate Subcommittee on Anti-Trust and Monopoly since 1957. Philip Hart, another Democrat, but one more friendly toward professional sports, assumed the chairmanship of the subcommittee upon Kefauver's death. When Hart was a student at the University of Michigan, his roommate had been Walter "Spike" Briggs, whose family owned the Detroit Tigers. Several years later Hart married Spike's sister and became a member of the Briggs family. Before entering politics, Hart served in the front offices of the Tigers and NFL Detroit Lions organizations. Aside from these important personal connections to the professional sports world, Hart brought a kinder and gentler tone to antitrust issues in general. He once said that he did not "believe in the gang-buster technique" of conducting antitrust investigations. One writer characterized Hart as the "gentlemanly trust-buster."[2]

Organized baseball had diffused much of the controversy surrounding itself when it effected the expansions of the American and National leagues in 1961 and 1962. Yet, the antitrust anomaly that had been created in the 1950s survived into the 1960s. Wielding the power of the chairmanship, Senator Hart introduced a bill containing his solution to the antitrust and professional sports issue.

S. 2391, or the Hart bill, was nearly identical to the old Keating bill that had passed the House in 1958; that is, the Hart bill was designed to place all professional team sports under the antitrust laws, but with automatic exemptions for practices relating to the equalization of competitive playing strengths, the employment, selection, or eligibility of players and their contracts, the right to operate within a certain geographic territory, and any practice relating to the preservation of public confidence in the honesty of sports contests.[3] Hart's bill was co-sponsored by Senator Keating and

45

Senator Edward Kennedy of Massachusetts. Hart believed, correctly, that professional sports would continually be plagued by antitrust litigation and uncertainty until Congress legislated a consistent place for them under the antitrust laws. He hoped his bill would do just that.

The Senate held four days of hearings on the Hart bill in January and February 1964. The chairman opened the hearings with the opinion that "During the past 5 years too many foul balls have been hit into the stands. It's about time that Congress connected with a legislative home run."[4] Following Hart's opening statement, the subcommittee listened to the testimony of Commissioner Ford Frick. This visit to Congress was Frick's thirteenth in as many years as baseball's commissioner, and his advice to Congress had not changed since 1951. "Our position then and now is that Organized Baseball through the years has evolved a system of self-regulation which, without being perfect, has served the public and the game," Frick declared. He also believed that all the professional team sports deserved "equal treatment under the law," and that the best way to accomplish that goal was through the Hart bill.[5]

Frick's statement contained nothing new; it was not a surprise that baseball would support the Hart bill, inasmuch as it had actively lobbied for the Keating bill in 1958. Both Hart and Frick could take added comfort in the fact that the players association concurred with Frick's analysis. Representatives for the players testified that the consensus among their colleagues was that the reserve clause was necessary and that the players were "fully in accord with the bill."[6]

Aside from the merits of the Hart bill, the commissioner was asked about another matter receiving a lot of publicity and causing general turmoil for the game. This matter involved a confrontation between Charles Finley, the brash owner of the Kansas City Athletics, and the rest of major league baseball's officialdom. Finley desperately wanted to move his team out of Kansas City, but the other owners overwhelmingly voted to block Finley's plans for a move. Frick seemed reluctant to discuss the matter, though he defended the major league's policy regarding franchise shifts, on the grounds that "leagues must be able to protect the game of baseball against irresponsible club owners . . . [and] the abuses of renegades."[7] Frick's characterization of Finley illustrated the depth of feeling involved in the controversy, which in many respects foreshadowed the problem the National Football League would have with Oakland Raiders owner Al Davis in the early 1980s. Davis, of course, would successfully move his team over the cries of the NFL, but because of their antitrust exemption, the major leagues were able to frustrate Finley's plans in 1964.

Beside the Finley controversy, there were few sparks in organized baseball's thirteenth visit with Congress. In fact, the 1964 hearings were probably the most cordial since the first Celler subcommittee inquiry in 1951.

Representatives from the other professional team sports were also called to testify on the Hart bill. The National Football League sent Commissioner Alvin "Pete" Rozelle and Ordell Braase, president of the National Football League Players Association. Rozelle sang only praises for the bill, characterizing it as "an informed and intelligent response to a situation which requires legislative action."[8]

Braase was not as sure about the merits of the Hart bill; many players, he said, were concerned that the bill would grant league owners too broad an antitrust exemption. They were also upset over the recent introduction of the Rozelle Rule, which allowed the commissioner to determine the compensation, in the form of a player of comparable worth, that a team signing a free agent had to pay the team losing the free agent. Braase argued that the Rozelle Rule discouraged player movement and free agency. His complaint fell mostly on deaf ears, however, as Senator Hart pointed out to Braase that baseball players operated under a perpetual reserve clause that allowed virtually no player movement, yet they supported his bill.[9] Braase and the rest of the NFL's players would have to wait another ten years before they received a sympathetic hearing on the Rozelle Rule.

The subcommittee also heard testimony from Walter Kennedy, commissioner of the National Basketball Association, and Clarence Campbell, commissioner of the National Hockey League. Both league commissioners wholeheartedly supported the Hart bill as in the "national interest." Campbell informed the subcommittee that there was currently only one native-born U.S. citizen playing in the NHL.[10] If nothing else, the subcommittee got a crash course on professional ice hockey and was reminded why Congress had paid so little attention to the game in the past.

The 1964 hearings were brief and in some ways premature, in that Congress was unlikely to take legislative action until organized baseball had the opportunity to solve its own problems regarding Charles Finley. Although the Hart bill was reported to the floor by the full Judiciary Committee, the bill was, nevertheless, doomed in the summer of 1964. For, in the second week of August, the New York Yankees were purchased by the Columbia Broadcasting System for the price of $11.2 million.[11]

The transaction made congressmen, the sports world, and the public pause to reflect upon the changes that professional sports had undergone during the previous fifteen years. The deal brought together the most successful and powerful baseball club in major league history and one of the mightiest broadcasting networks in the country. Apart from the obvious antitrust implications of the transaction, some were upset with it because they believed the major leagues had somehow sold out to the television industry, an industry that seemed to be gobbling up everything in its path, including the minor leagues. One observer sarcastically pointed out that CBS, owner of the Beverly Hillbillies, was also the owner of the most powerful team in baseball. To some fans, the deal seemed almost blasphemous.

The transaction was one of the factors leading to a new perception of professional sports as basically profit-oriented businesses rather than idyllic pastimes. Any chance that the Hart bill had for passage in the summer of 1964 was torpedoed by the CBS-Yankees deal; congressmen clamored for more hearings to discuss the antitrust implications of the ownership of a major league ball club by a broadcast network.

Disappointed but undaunted, Senator Hart reintroduced his bill early in 1965. The 1965 version of the Hart bill was identical to the previous year's offering; that is, S. 950 would legislate a place for all of professional team sports under the antitrust laws, but grant them automatic exemption for such things as the reserve clause, territorial rights, and the powers of the commissioner. These practices, the bill explained, were "unique to organized league activity and necessary for the survival of professional team sports."[12] In sum, the Hart bill attempted to distinguish between those elements of professional sports that were a blend of sports and business, and those elements that were purely business. Hart believed that the latter needed to be under the antitrust laws, but that the former deserved an exemption. Of course, partly because of the CBS-Yankees deal, the lines between "sport" practices and "business" practices were increasingly difficult to identify, and many in Congress were concerned that the exemptions offered in the Hart bill were too generous.

Hearings were scheduled in late February 1965 to debate the Hart bill in light of the CBS-Yankees transaction. The subcommittee was particularly interested in the advantages that CBS and the Yankees might have gained over their competitors as a result of their new relationship. Many congressmen feared that CBS would have the upper hand in the periodic bidding war with the National Broadcasting Company and the American Broadcasting Company over the network rights to televise major league games. Others expressed a fear that CBS affiliates in the New York territory would replace the independent networks that had held the broadcasting rights to local telecasts of Yankees games. As for the Yankees, some argued that they, already the most powerful major league franchise, would now be in an even better position to dictate policy to the other teams.

Dr. Frank Stanton, president of CBS, was called before the subcommittee to discuss these issues. Stanton explained to the subcommittee that the operations of the Yankees were completely separate from those of CBS and were controlled by the president of the ball club, Daniel Topping. As for the notion that CBS might gain an unfair advantage in the network bidding war for package contracts, Stanton believed that such an advantage would not be realized because the entire league approved package deals, not one team.

Stanton also assured the subcommittee that CBS had no plans to use its affiliates in the New York area to supplant the local broadcast agreements the Yankees currently held with independent broadcast stations. He admitted that such a thing was possible in theory, but argued that it was impractical because the CBS affiliates in the New York area would have to sacrifice their regular prime-time lineup, something CBS would not allow its affiliates to do. Stanton concluded that the reason CBS purchased the Yankees was because the network "admired the club's winning ways . . . [and] thought it was a good investment." In general, Stanton worked hard to convince the congressmen that the two operations would remain independent, and that neither CBS nor the Yankees had gained a monopolistic advantage.[13]

Representing baseball for the fourteenth time, Commissioner Frick testified in support of the CBS-Yankees deal and the Hart bill. He also assured the subcommittee that the operations of the network and team would be separate; he, as commissioner, would not allow CBS to be "placed in any favored position as owner of the Yankees."

As for the Hart bill, Frick still believed that it offered the best solution to the inconsistent situation of professional team sports under the antitrust laws.[14]

Other major league officials agreed with Frick. Joseph Cronin, president of the American League, testified concerning the CBS-Yankees deal that "all the money in the world cannot play first base or shortstop—Gentlemen this game of baseball is a game of ability."[15] The Yankees would soon bear out Cronin's analysis, as they tumbled from the top of the American League to mediocrity in the late 1960s.

Others in organized baseball were more cautious about the CBS-Yankees deal. Although he was unable, or unwilling, to testify in 1964, Charles Finley did appear before the subcommittee during the 1965 hearings. The subcommittee had been eager to discuss his past problems with the municipal officials in Kansas City and officials in organized baseball. Senator Edward V. Long, a Democrat from Missouri, had tried to get Finley and his financial records subpoenaed during the 1964 hearings.[16] Finley came before the subcommittee in 1965 of his own accord, however.

He echoed all of the concerns over the CBS-Yankees deal that had been bandied about since the deal's consummation. Finley told the subcommittee that CBS would have an advantage in bidding for telecast rights because it would be privy to information about the American League, to which the other networks would not have access. He also felt that the Yankees would be much too powerful vis-à-vis the other teams in the league as a result of the deal. He predicted that CBS and its Yankees would "call the tune, and seven others will dance." Finley was referring to the seven team owners who, together with the Yankees, voted to approve the team's sale. Indeed, the owners approved the sale by a vote of eight to two; Finley, of course, was in the minority. But Finley had a bone to pick with all of organized baseball, and his dissent from the majority viewpoint surprised no one.[17]

Indeed, the consensus among the witnesses was that Congress did not need to fret over the CBS-Yankees deal. Other witnesses testified in support of the transaction. Walter Kennedy, commissioner of the NBA, not only viewed the deal as harmless, but fully endorsed the Hart bill. Pete Rozelle and Clarence Campbell testified that the National Football League and the National Hockey League supported both the sale of the Yankees and the Hart bill.[18]

Moreover, representatives from the other two major networks testified in favor of the CBS-Yankees deal and the Hart bill. Thomas Moore, president of ABC, said that any perceived conflict of interest would only serve to keep CBS honest. Julian Goodman of NBC echoed Moore's testimony, adding that, while NBC held no immediate plans to purchase a team, it might decide to in the future and would not feel any particular conflict of interest in doing so.[19] Thus, with the exception of the disgruntled Charles Finley, the witnesses before the subcommittee supported the legality of the CBS-Yankees relationship and the Hart bill as well.

In 1965 the Hart bill was not only reported favorably to the floor of the Senate, but was actually passed by a voice vote on August 31.[20] The bill failed to reach the floor of the House of Representatives for a vote before the first session of the 89th Congress concluded. Thus, two versions of the same sports bill had passed each house of Congress, but in different decades. Representative Keating had guided an antitrust bill successfully through the House in 1958 and Senator Hart had done so in 1965. But despite the efforts of Keating and Hart and seven legislative hearings over fourteen years, Congress had failed to legislate a coherent, consistent position for professional team sports under the antitrust laws.

Congress would not again take up the issue of the baseball antitrust anomaly until the early 1970s. That decade brought great changes in organized baseball, but in 1972, in *Flood v. Kuhn*, the Supreme Court upheld the status quo in regard to the reserve clause. In the latest case involving a challenge to the reserve clause and baseball's antitrust exemption, the court admitted that baseball represented an "exception," "aberration," and "anomaly." But the court added, "If there is any inconsistency or illogic in all this, it is an inconsistency and illogic of long standing that is to be remedied by the Congress and not by this Court."

It is interesting to note that as an introduction to the majority opinion, Justice Harry Blackmun felt compelled to offer a brief history of the game, including a long list of baseball greats that stretched from Ty Cobb to Dizzy Dean.[21] Yet, as far as the federal judiciary was concerned, any correction of the baseball anomaly would have to come from within organized baseball through collective bargaining or from Congress through legislation. The "jurisdictional volleyball" continued.

In the wake of the *Flood* decision and numerous other points of instability within the professional sports world, including controversy over professional football's blackout policies and the proposed merger of the NBA and the American Basketball Association, the Senate held hearings in the summer of 1972 on a bill aimed at creating a federal sports commission. Introduced by Senator Marlow W. Cook of Kentucky, the bill would have established an eleven-man commission within the Department of Commerce to oversee professional sports. The commission would have concerned itself with practices such as broadcasting, the sale and transfer of franchises, drafts, territorial rights, and player contracts.[22] Such a commission, Cook believed, could remove the inequities and injustices that existed in and between the professional team sports in relation to the antitrust laws.

Four days of hearings were scheduled to debate the idea of a federal sports commission. The commissioners from the various professional team sports one by one spoke out against the bill. Bowie Kuhn, commissioner of baseball since 1969, told the senators that baseball could solve its own labor problems through good faith bargaining, and that a federal sports commission was neither appropriate nor necessary.[23] Pete Rozelle, football's commissioner, agreed with Kuhn, arguing that the various professional sports were unique and an umbrella-type agency could not effectively manage professional team sports.[24] Commissioner Walter Kennedy of the NBA also testified against the bill, but primarily used his time before the subcommittee to drum up support for the proposed NBA-ABA merger.[25] In sum, all of professional team sports officialdom opposed the Cook bill and perceived it more as a threat than a solution to their antitrust problems.

One witness who disagreed with the commissioners of the various professional sports was ABC sportscaster Howard Cosell. This visit would be the first of many for Cosell before congressional subcommittees. In 1972 Cosell spoke out strongly in support of the Cook bill. Cosell argued that professional sports had become big businesses and that they did not need antitrust exemption, but federal regulation. "Make no mistake about it," Cosell would later write, "baseball is a business." He added that the game's attempt to cloak itself in "Americanism and Patriotism" was "almost obscene." One report called him the "star" of the hearings; indeed, Cosell attracted a crowd to the hearing room in the same way that Casey Stengel and

Branch Rickey had in earlier years.[26] Yet, for all of Cosell's "hammering" testimony and notoriety, the Cook bill failed to reach the floor of the Senate, and the professional sports world escaped unscathed from another encounter with Congress.

The next congressional inquiry dealing with the baseball anomaly came in 1975. Great changes had occurred within organized baseball between 1972 and 1975. Much has been written about organized baseball's labor-management struggles in the mid-1970s.[27] It is sufficient to say here that through the arbitration cases of players, particularly Dave McNally and Andy Messersmith, organized baseball developed a new labor arrangement that took a lot of bite out of the reserve clause. Simply, the perpetual reserve clause was replaced by a six-year reserve clause, followed by free agency. As the average major league career is less than six years, it is debatable just how much the new agreement weakened the reserve clause. Nevertheless, the fact is that both the players and the club owners felt the need to retain some sort of reserve system, and both sides were satisfied with the six-year limit.[28] The players had achieved for themselves what neither the courts nor Congress had been willing to give them.

Yet, Congress continued to attempt to legislate a place for professional team sports under the antitrust laws. Two bills were introduced into the House of Representatives in 1975 with the intent of outlawing all labor reserve systems in professional sports. In October 1975, four hours of hearings were held by what was now called the House Subcommittee on Monopolies and Commercial Law. The hearings focused entirely on the reserve system in use by professional football, particularly the Rozelle Rule, which had recently come under fire in the courts through the case of *Kapp v. NFL*.[29]

Emanuel Celler, then 87 years old, testified in support of the proposed bills because he felt it was time for Congress to "loosen the fetters that bind [the] employees in this last significant unregulated monopoly."[30] Although the bills, if passed, would have had a direct bearing on all professional team sports, the sub-committee did not hear testimony from any representatives of organized baseball, professional basketball, or professional hockey. As for the bills, they produced nothing other than the four hours of legislative hearings.

The next congressional investigation into professional sports also failed to produce legislation, but it did produce a great deal more publicity and more than 1,000 pages of testimony. In 1976 the House created the Select Committee on Professional Sports to examine the state of affairs in football, basketball, hockey, and baseball. Special or select committee investigations differ from typical hearings or investigations in several ways. They are not called to debate specific legislation, but rather they are temporary, created to examine a particular matter and suggest a legislative course of action. Often, they are called in response to a public feeling that Congress "should do something" about an urgent problem or issue. Some of the best-known congressional committees have been of this type, such as the Senate Watergate Committee of 1973 and the House and Senate committees on the Iran-Contra affair.[31]

The changes in professional sports had been profound, and some believed that baseball's labor disputes, basketball's failed merger, football's antitrust litigation, increasing violence in hockey, and rumored franchise relocations in basketball and hockey warranted a special investigation by Congress. As Representative B.F. Sisk of California summarized the motive behind the hearing, "To put it mildly, the sports world seems turned on its head." Though the select committee was not called to debate legislation, it would "produce a reasoned articulation of the problems facing professional sports, and set a direction toward constructive legislation."[32]

The hearings produced a lot of fresh, if not original, testimony. Baseball's commissioner, Bowie Kuhn, came to the stand in 1976 armed with the game's new labor agreement. After explaining the new arrangement to the members of the committee, he proceeded to argue for baseball's continued antitrust exemption on the grounds that the game's conduct had been responsible and the current situation did not justify any action by the federal government.[33] Committee members had a hard time disagreeing with Kuhn in light of recent developments within organized baseball. Kuhn suggested that the best thing for professional sports generally would be for Congress to grant them complete antitrust exemption.[34] Except for the 1951 hearings, organized baseball had never appeared more confident before Congress.

Another baseball representative agreed with Kuhn. M. Donald Grant, president of the New York Mets, argued that the national pastime deserved continued antitrust exemption because, in addition to its new labor arrangement, it was "the only sport left in America where a father of a family can, on any given Saturday morning, say,

'Children, would you like to go and see Tom Seaver pitch?'" Grant praised baseball for offering the highest number of games to sports fans at the cheapest ticket prices, and argued that such behavior warranted continued antitrust exemption.[35]

Richard Dozer, sportswriter for the *Chicago Tribune* and president of the Baseball Writers Association of America, heartily agreed with baseball officials. Dozer supported the reserve clause because "they [the players] have the right to leave and sell shoes, build bridges, or drive trucks. . . . I think some of them demanded really a little too much."[36] From Dozer's view, the players were the villains rather than the downtrodden victims. (Undoubtedly, a sizable slice of the public, sick of listening to baseball players' demands, concurred with Dozer's sentiments.)

Another writer, the renowned novelist James A. Michener, also the author of *Sports in America*, testified on behalf of baseball. Respected not only for his writing talent but for his knowledge of sports, Michener defended the status quo on sociopolitical grounds. He claimed that sports "are a major factor in modern society, whether the society is democratic or totalitarian. The nation that does well in sports gets the advantage." Michener cited East Germany as a prime example. He concluded that the best course of action for Congress would be to offer exemption for the four major sports, although he did feel that they all needed to be placed on equal footing under the antitrust laws.[37]

The select committee also heard from officials of the other three team sports. Pete Rozelle of the NFL, Clarence Campbell of the NHL, and Lawrence O'Brien, commissioner of the NBA, were grilled about the problems afflicting their particular sports, but each one supported Kuhn's position on the antitrust laws—complete exemption could be the panacea for their sport's illnesses.[38]

Although the majority of the witnesses argued for antitrust exemptions, a significant number did not. Marvin Miller, executive director of the Major League Baseball Players Association, and Edward R. Garvey, who held the same position with the National Football League Players Association, pleaded with Congress to refrain from granting any additional antitrust exemptions to professional sports. Although Miller had been able to lead baseball players to free agency, he told the committee that the fight was long and grueling because of the game's antitrust exemption. He also warned that if professional football were given a similar exemption, players of the gridiron would be stripped of whatever power they had attained through their union and their prospects for free agency would drop dramatically.[39]

Naturally, Garvey agreed with Miller. He told the committee to "ignore the hollow phrases that have been used to justify the reserve system over the past several decades." The "villain," Garvey continued, was not the so-called greedy athlete, but the "intransigence of the NFL owners." He concluded that further antitrust exemption for professional sports would only be injurious to the careers of professional athletes.[40]

Although sportswriter Dozer and author Michener supported the exemption route, another sports commentator did not. In fact, Howard Cosell, amid a packed hearing room, had little good to say about the hierarchy of organized baseball and professional sports generally. Once again, Cosell clearly placed himself on the side of the players, favoring the removal of baseball's antitrust exemption. Cosell pointed to "the basic inconsistency" whereby "baseball would like singly and alone in the United States of America to be the one business free of and above the law." Cosell believed that complete application of the antitrust laws was the best medicine for what ailed professional sports.[41]

The select committee, however, was less certain than its witnesses about the proper course of action Congress needed to take. One committee member claimed that the investigation was "done without a full comprehensive look at the whole subject of antitrust."[42] The rest of the committee concurred as the hearings drew to a close. The select committee reported that there was not really sufficient evidence to warrant a continuation of baseball's antitrust exemption, but also recommended that Congress refrain from acting on the matter until a more thorough investigation could be completed.[43] Thus, 28 hearing sessions, 89 witnesses, 1,200 pages of testimony, and a 700-page report produced nothing other than a recommendation for more of the same.

The colossal, but fruitless, 1976 congressional inquiry into professional sports was the last major effort of that decade by Congress to correct the baseball anomaly. In the early 1980s, however, Congress took up the question once again, though in a much more limited way. Hearings were held in 1981 and stretched into 1982 on the issue of organized baseball's historic exemption from the antitrust laws. Three days were given to the baseball anomaly in hearings that were ostensibly called to pick up where the 1976 select committee left off.

Commissioner Bowie Kuhn and player representative Marvin Miller clashed over the antitrust issue in 1981–82 as they had done in 1976. Kuhn predictably pointed to the sport's honorable tradition of self-regulation and again prodded Congress to grant complete antitrust immunity to the other professional sports. When asked about the game's recent long and painful player strike, Kuhn claimed that it had nothing to do with the sport's antitrust exemption. He also complained to the subcommittee that the game was suffering because of the exorbitant salaries being paid to free agents. The game was losing money, said Kuhn, and if something was not done, the national pastime's days could be numbered.[44]

Marvin Miller scoffed at Kuhn's sob story. Stories of poverty in the game had been "going on for decades." Referring to the owners' unwillingness to surrender their teams' financial records, Miller added, "You have to be more than a little suspicious of poverty claims that are unauthenticated."[45] Indeed, the entire antitrust and professional sports debate had been "going on for decades" and would continue to do so, because the 1981–82 congressional hearings once again failed to produce legislative fruit.

Although Congress concerned itself with other issues in professional sports during the 1980s, especially franchise relocations and broadcasting policies, it did not readdress the baseball anomaly in any significant way until the early 1990s. In December 1992 Congress again picked up the issue of baseball's antitrust exemption. As usual, a number of problems within the sport presented congressmen with the opportunity to call for hearings. The 1992 hearings were called because of the alleged racial slurs of Cincinnati Reds owner Marge Schott, the firing of baseball Commissioner Francis "Fay" Vincent, and the attempted move of the Giants franchise from San Francisco to the Tampa Bay area.

During the relatively brief hearings held by the Senate Judiciary Committee, congressmen listened to testimony from Fay Vincent and interim Commissioner Bud Selig. Selig, of course, argued for the continuation of baseball's exemption and assured the congressmen that organized baseball was handling the Schott affair and the proposed Giants' move in the best way possible. He also pointed to the National League's addition of two more teams for the 1993 season as evidence that the game was acting in the public interest.

Vincent, on the other hand, was not as confident where the owners were concerned. He suggested that Congress wait until after the selection of the new commissioner before determining the game's antitrust fate. If the powers of the new commissioner were diminished, Vincent believed, the game's exemption should be removed, but he was willing to take a wait-and-see attitude before calling for complete application of the antitrust laws. Vincent generally received a sympathetic hearing before the Senate subcommittee, and Senator Howard Metzenbaum of Ohio agreed with Vincent that the owners did not want a strong commissioner, but a "cruise director for their cartel."[46] Yet for all of Metzenbaum's rhetoric, no legislation came close to passing in 1992.

* * *

So organized baseball's unique position under the nation's antitrust laws has remained unchanged since 1922. Moreover, it was the Supreme Court, not Congress, that granted this privileged position to organized baseball. The game's exemption originated in the *Federal League* case of 1922. The Supreme Court upheld the 1922 decision in the *Toolson* case of 1953 and, most recently, in the *Flood* case of 1972. Although the Court has not always exercised such restraint and deference to Congress, in baseball matters it has consistently yielded to the legislative branch. Congress, nonetheless, has consistently refused to legislate a clear position for organized baseball and the other professional team sports under the antitrust laws.

In fact, 40 years, a dozen hearings, scores of bills, and hundreds of witnesses have produced little more than thousands of pages of recorded testimony and committee reports. Few pieces of legislation have come close to becoming law; indeed, most of the proposed bills never made it out of the subcommittees in which they were debated. Thus, any influence that Congress has had on baseball has been indirect. For example, Congress can accept some of the credit for the game's westward expansion in 1961–62. But population shifts and improvements in transportation may have had as much to do with this inevitable development as any action taken by the legislature. As for the reserve clause, one must agree with James B. Dworkin: "[I]t can be said that were it not for the grievance/arbitration procedure, baseball's former reserve system would probably have remained intact to date."[47]

A number of factors have led to Congress's inaction regarding organized baseball. Each congressional attempt to legislate a consistent place for professional team sports failed because of particular circumstances. But the transcending factor that has allowed the baseball anomaly to survive is the image that the game has cultivated as the American national pastime. All of the hearings, from 1951 to 1992, had at least one thing in common: they all contained numerous references to the romance and nostalgia that are so much a part of the game of baseball. The significance and power of such statements cannot be overestimated, particularly for the first twenty years of the Congress-organized baseball relationship. The statements of Ty Cobb, Casey Stengel, Branch Rickey, Ford Frick, and Bowie Kuhn have proven extremely effective in buttressing the image of baseball. The reality is that few other American institutions, including the other professional sports, are surrounded by the profound romantic aura that envelops the institution of organized baseball.

Baseball's armor of nostalgia was at its strongest in the first two decades of its involvement with Congress. Words such as *clean, honest, integrity, honor, patriotic,* and *national* were used over and over to characterize the sport. It is true that during that period, baseball's romance was not strong enough to move Congress to grant it legislative exemption from the antitrust laws. But the sport's image did protect it from legislation that threatened to place baseball under the antitrust laws. The status quo was maintained and, for organized baseball, that meant exemption from the antitrust laws. Clearly, the game's romantic aura serves as the best explanation for Congress's paralysis during the period 1951–71.

The romance of the game also explains, at least in part, Congress's inaction over the last twenty years. By the early 1970s the game's image—and the image of professional sports generally—had become less idyllic and more businesslike. Baseball's image had been affected by the CBS-Yankees deal, player discontent, and the arbitration/grievance cases of such players as McNally, Messersmith, and Jim "Catfish" Hunter. But baseball is still considered by many, if not all, to be the "American game."

Thus, as late as 1972 the Supreme Court not only upheld baseball's exemption in the *Flood* case, but also prefaced the majority opinion with references to the heroes and traditions of the game. The advent of free agency made the issue of baseball's exemption less urgent, but it is difficult to argue with Dworkin on this matter. If free agency had not been achieved through collective bargaining, baseball would probably still be operating with a perpetual reserve clause. There is no real evidence to suggest that either Congress or the increasingly conservative Supreme Court would have removed the game's antitrust exemption in the interest of free agency.

To be sure, Congress has acted boldly since 1970 with the other professional sports. The antiblackout legislation in 1973 and the defeat of the basketball merger in 1972 are good examples of congressional action. But with regard to organized baseball, Congress has remained in the stands. In fact, while the game's image may have changed from one of a sport first and a business second to a business first and a sport second, baseball's privileged position under the nation's antitrust laws has remained unscathed over the last 40 years. After all the hearings, witnesses, legal arguments, and reports, what member of Congress would seriously consider any piece of legislation that might threaten the "American game" played by the "kid on the sandlot"?

Chapter 5

The Red-Light District, 1960–85

In the 1920s and 1930s, professional boxing was largely successful in rehabilitating its public image, but by the 1940s the game was coming under renewed attack from commentators and legislators. As early as the spring of 1940, U.S. Representative Ambrose Kennedy of Maryland introduced a bill to create a federal boxing commission for the purpose of ridding the sport of any possible criminal elements.[1] After the reign of Joe Louis ended eight years later, the sport's image began another downward spiral.

Then, in 1955, James D. Norris's International Boxing Club, the organization that effectively took the place of the defunct Twentieth Century Sporting Club and controlled the lion's share of professional bouts, found itself before the U.S. Supreme Court on charges of monopoly. Some thought that the Court would treat professional boxing the same way it had organized baseball in the *Toolson* case a couple of years earlier. By a margin of seven to two, however, the court decided in *U.S. v IBC* that professional boxing belonged under the antitrust laws.

In writing the minority opinion, Justice Felix Frankfurter claimed that, if baseball deserved an antitrust exemption, so did boxing.[2] But while the "great American sport" represented everything that was good about America, boxing conjured up images of urban vice, gambling, and generally all that was wrong with America.[3] Thus, the Court placed the sport under the Sherman Act and ordered the IBC to disband.

Although the IBC was liquidated, the dark side of professional boxing remained as mobsters and rumors of fixes continued to plague the sport. In August 1959 California Governor Edmund G. Brown declared that the sport "smells to high heaven," and that boxing would remain legal in his state only if cleansed by a federal investigation.[4] Arthur Daley of the *New York Times* commented that the boxing industry had "an unholy fascination for the mobsters, the racket guys and the low-lifes. . . . Boxing is the slum-area of sports and the forces of evil have thus far been able to prevent all attempts at clearance or rehabilitation."[5]

Senator Estes Kefauver recognized an opportunity to place his antitrust subcommittee in the public eye and scheduled hearings on professional boxing for the summer of 1960. Kefauver, of course, was also busy that summer with organized baseball and the Continental League, but he felt that the subcommittee's involvement with another professional sport would shine even more light on his trustbusting activities. Kefauver was not a stranger to the evils of professional boxing or the underworld. His famous investigation of organized crime in 1950-51 had delved into the latter at some length, taking testimony from the likes of "Trigger Mike," the "Enforcer," "Little Big Man," and "Jimmy Blue Eyes."[6] The 1950–51 crime investigation was televised in many areas of the country. Besides proving that organized crime was active in American society in the 1950s, the investigation helped solidify Kefauver's reputation on the national level as a hard-nosed senator looking out for John Q. Public.[7]

As they had done in 1950, critics argued that the senator from Tennessee was avoiding the issues that really concerned the public by choosing "the path where the publicity, votes, and campaign funds might be found."[8] Publicity was undoubtedly important to Kefauver, who was embroiled in a close reelection race with Republican candidate Judge Andrew T. Taylor.[9] Thus, Kefauver ignored his critics, gambled that the hearings on boxing would generate more good publicity than bad, and proceeded with his plans to investigate the monopolistic and criminal elements of boxing.

Kefauver was so busy with his reelection bid in the summer of 1960, however, that he placed Senator Philip Hart in charge of the boxing hearings when they opened on June 14. In his opening statement, Hart cited Governor Brown's concerns, the convictions of Frankie Carbo and several other mobsters who had ties to the sport, and the *U.S. v IBC* case as reasons for the hearings. Hart explained that the hearings would determine whether "corrective Federal legislation is warranted."[10] The subcommittee secured the services of John Bonomi to aid in the questioning of witnesses. Bonomi, assistant district attorney of New York County and a participant in cases involving the New York State Athletic Commission and boxing in the late 1950s, would do most of the questioning in the 1960 investigation.[11]

The first part of the hearings, held on June 14 and 15, gathered as much information as possible concerning the monopolistic and criminal aspects of the sport, specifically about Frankie Carbo. Carbo, who was serving a two-year prison term at Riker's Island Prison for a conviction for undercover managing and matchmaking, was the underworld boss of the sport. With the help of an assistant named Frank "Blinky" Palermo and a deal struck with James D. Norris, Carbo wielded significant control over the fight game in the 1950s.[12] He had a long history of trouble with legal authorities that included seventeen arrests for everything from vagrancy to grand larceny to murder. Carbo's influence on the sport was the primary focus of the hearings.

The first witness called in June was former middleweight champion Jacob "Jake" LaMotta. For the first time publicly, LaMotta told the story of how he had thrown his fight with Billy Fox in the fall of 1947 in order to get a shot at the middleweight title. Speaking in a low tone, the "Bronx Bull" claimed that he had been offered $100,000 to throw the fight, but that he had refused to accept the money and demanded a title shot instead. Although LaMotta denied Palermo's connection to the Fox fight in his testimony, he had admitted Palermo's involvement in a statement previously given to Bonomi during a New York state investigation. LaMotta also denied that he was unwilling to implicate known mobsters out of fear for his life. He also told the subcommittee that he had been offered $100,000 to throw a fight with Tony Janiro a few months before his bout with Fox in 1947, but that he refused to accept the money because he was interested solely in the title.[13]

LaMotta recounted how he was forced to endure a two-year "cooling-off" period before he received his title shot. He got his chance in the summer of 1949 when he signed to fight the middleweight champion, Marcel Cerdan. Although his purse was only $19,000, LaMotta testified, he was forced to pay Cerdan's manager $20,000 for the opportunity. (He also informed the subcommittee, however, that he bet on himself and ended up making $16,000 on the fight.)[14] LaMotta concluded his two-hour testimony by claiming that his experience in the sport was not the exception, but the rule. He admitted that racketeers exerted a great influence in boxing; although he despised such "bums" and "rats," the road to success and the title passed through the criminal elements; and one had to cooperate with the Frankie Carbos and Blinky Palermos.[15] He later wrote that he hoped his testimony contributed "in some way . . . to cleansing the cesspool that boxing is being drowned in."[16]

The subcommittee also listened to testimony from Jake's brother, Joseph LaMotta. Joey was Jake's manager at the time of the Cerdan fight and, although he refused to admit it, was involved in the bribe offer connected with the Janiro fight and the $20,000 payment for the Cerdan fight.[17] Despite a great deal of persistence, Bonomi was unable to get Joey to link any underworld figure, much less Frankie Carbo, to the fight scene. Like a number of others who followed him, Joey LaMotta pleaded the Fifth Amendment repeatedly and refused to implicate any known criminals.[18]

The initial phase of the Senate hearings on professional boxing lasted only two days. Jake LaMotta's testimony had been the most publicized aspect of hearings that had produced nothing in the way of legislative recommendations. But the hearings had confirmed what many believed; that is, "Fixes and rumors of fixes, clandestine deals and infiltration by mobsters have characterized boxing ever since it became a business in the '20s." As the sports world looked to the next round of hearings scheduled for December, one commentator hoped that the subcommittee would use its "excellent opportunity" to go after "lasting results, not quick headlines," because "Americans still love a good prize fight."[19]

Round two of the U.S. Senate's investigation into professional boxing stretched over five days in December 1960. The second installment of the investigation differed from the first in that Senator Kefauver chaired the proceedings and a bill, drafted by Senator Alexander Wiley of Wisconsin, was before the subcommittee. The bill, S. 3690, sought to prohibit racketeers from being licensed as promoters, matchmakers, or managers.[20] The hearings were supposed to pick up where the hearings of the previous June had left off. Wiley assured boxing fans at the outset that the hearings and his bill were designed to "cure the patient, not to kill him."[21] So far, at least, the subcommittee felt that the sport only needed to be cleansed and not abolished.

The hearings of December 1960 contained the testimony of a number of controversial and shadowy figures. The subcommittee had been waiting to discuss the issue with witnesses such as James D. Norris, Blinky Palermo, and Frankie Carbo ever since their names surfaced in the June hearings. The public, too, was extraordinarily interested in what these men had to say. Unfortunately for the public and the legislators, most of the pivotal witnesses said little.

One important witness who was relatively forthcoming was the former IBC boss, James D. Norris. Considerable controversy surrounded Norris's testimony, partly because Senator Kefauver had charged that Norris was attempting to avoid appearing before the subcommittee. Norris did drag his feet, claiming ill health as the reason for his reluctance to testify. Ultimately, an agreement was reached with Norris and his physician whereby Norris would testify before the subcommittee in a closed session in order to ease any tension on his heart.[22] One report described Norris on the day of his testimony as "wearing a somber tan and a funeral suit. . . . [He] walked with the reluctant step of a man approaching the gallows. . . . Indeed, the jig was up."[23]

Norris, who at one time owned stock in Detroit's Olympia Stadium, New York's Madison Square Garden, the St. Louis Arena, and Chicago Stadium, related to the senators how he and the rest of the IBC had developed a relationship with known racketeers, primarily Frankie Carbo. Essentially, Norris and the IBC controlled the sites, licensing, and media contracts, while Frankie Carbo controlled the matchmakers, managers, and fighters.[24] Together, Norris and Carbo monopolized professional boxing. Norris testified that the IBC quickly realized that if it was going to survive, it needed to develop a working relationship with certain racketeers, Carbo being the foremost. Norris recounted how the IBC funneled money to Carbo by placing the racketeer's girlfriend, Viola Masters, on the IBC's payroll. In exchange, Carbo served the IBC as a "convincer" and "expediter" in setting up major fights involving the likes of former champions Jake LaMotta, Carmen Basilio, Tony De Marco, and Willie Pep.

Norris seemed remorseful in his appearance and told the subcommittee that he was "embarrassed" by the IBC's relationship with Carbo. He defended his actions on the grounds that such a relationship was necessary to produce quality fights. He had upset Carbo and others in 1952 by offering J. Edgar Hoover $1 million to serve as the head of the IBC for ten years and to clean up the sport. Federal intervention, Norris believed, was the only thing that could "save boxing." Senator Kefauver chastised Norris for getting involved with the underworld, but praised his testimony for its forthrightness.[25]

Truman Gibson, Norris's right-hand man in the operation of the IBC, also testified before the subcommittee. At the time of his appearance, Gibson, along with Carbo and Palermo, was under indictment in California for allegedly conspiring to steal the fight purse of former welterweight champion Don Jordan. Gibson echoed much of what Norris had said, recounting to the subcommittee how Viola Masters rather than Carbo was paid approximately $45,000 because her name "looked better on our records." He also stated that the IBC had paid $27,500 to Jack Kearns, head of the International Boxing Managers Guild, to insure a free flow of fighters. Gibson, a University of Chicago graduate, generally told the story of how the IBC, working with Frankie Carbo, was able to monopolize the sport to the point that they controlled 45% of the championship fights between 1937 and 1949.[26] As Norris had done, Gibson predicted the death of the sport unless Congress stepped in to clean it up.[27]

Having heard from representatives of the IBC, the subcommittee turned next to the testimony of Frankie Carbo. Carbo's testimony was one of the most publicized in the history of the Congress–professional sports relationship. His attorney and two U.S. marshals escorted Carbo into the hearing room of the Old Senate Office Building.[28] At age 56, Carbo was in ill health, suffering from a kidney condition and diabetes; nevertheless, he still invoked fear in many associated with the fight game.[29] The senators asked Carbo dozens of questions relating to his involvement with professional boxing and each time he pleaded the Fifth Amendment. Following the subcommittee's numerous failures to ferret information out of Carbo, Senator Kefauver concluded by asking Carbo if he had anything else that he wanted to say. After conferring with his lawyer, Carbo responded, "There's only one thing that I would like to say— congratulations on your reelection."[30]

Beside Norris, Gibson, and Carbo, the subcommittee also listened to the testimony of the leading heavyweight contender in 1960, Charles "Sonny" Liston. The subcommittee called Liston to testify because rumor had it that he was under the unofficial control of racketeers. Although his manager of record was Joseph "Pep" Barone, many believed that Liston was actually controlled by organized crime figures, including Carbo and Blinky Palermo.

At 6' 1-1/2" and 212 pounds, Liston cut an impressive figure in the hearing room. Yet Liston's intellectual capacity failed to match his physical capacity, and his testimony added little to the hearings. He spent most of his time discussing his background. Liston testified that he was one of 25 children in a family that had survived by working in the cotton fields of Arkansas. He got into trouble with the authorities at the age of fourteen and spent much of the next thirteen years of his life in Missouri correctional facilities. He revealed his ignorance when he was asked by one subcommittee member if he knew what a check for $25,000 was worth. He responded that he did not know, and that he had to rely on others for the management of his financial affairs. Indeed, Liston could neither read nor write, beyond signing his name, and he was clearly an easy target for racketeers. Although he admitted to knowing Palermo on a personal level, Liston testified that he knew of no racketeers who were involved in his professional life. (In fact, the title contender was being controlled by the Carbo-Palermo team.)[31]

When asked by Senator Kefauver if men such as Blinky Palermo should be allowed to involve themselves with the sport of boxing, Liston responded, "Well, I couldn't pass judgement on no one, I haven't been perfect myself." The St. Louis authorities could vouch for that. As Liston concluded his testimony, Senator Kefauver claimed that the fighter "had a lot of good" in him, but urged him to get rid of any criminal influences on his career, lest he find himself in front of another congressional hearing in the future. When asked about the prospects of the sport and the need for legislation, Liston suggested, the "onliest thing that will bring it back to life is a guy that'll fight like Joe Louis, anybody and everybody and not just sit on the title."[32]

Another Joe Louis probably could have helped, but as the second round of congressional hearings on professional boxing came to a close, the senators were becoming more and more convinced that some form of federal legislation was necessary for the survival of the sport. As Kefauver said, "I am satisfied other members of the subcommittee agree that legislation must be passed to remove monopolistic influences. . . . Unless this is done . . . the sport might well pass from the American scene."[33] Kefauver suggested that the best course would be to create a temporary federal boxing commission with the power to grant licenses to promoters, managers, and fighters. He promised to have a bill of this nature ready for Congress by the end of the following January.

The senator from Tennessee kept his promise, introducing S. 1474, a bill to establish a federal boxing commission for the purpose of curbing monopolistic control of the sport. Two days of hearings on Kefauver's bill were scheduled in May and June 1961.

Enthusiasm among boxing's reformers was running high in the spring of 1961. Carbo, Palermo, and Gibson were found guilty in their California trials during February, receiving prison sentences ranging from 15 to 25 years. Moreover, Representative William Fitz Ryan of New York sponsored a bill in the House identical to Kefauver's; as the third round of congressional hearings approached, many observers in and out of Congress held high hopes for the passage of some boxing reform legislation.

Highlighting round three of Congress's bout with the boxing monopoly was a parade of former heavyweight champions. But before those stars could shine in the committee hearing room, the subcommittee listened to the statement of U.S. Senator Clair Engle of California. Engle had boxed as an amateur during his youth and was a co-sponsor of Kefauver's bill. Said Engle, "The cold facts [add] up to one conclusion: that in professional boxing today the question is not how good you are, but who you pay to prove how good you are." He recognized the "valiant efforts" that the state commissions had made to clean up a sport that was in a "low state of public opinion," but they needed help from the federal government. Congress, he continued, "does not hesitate to enact laws regulating other businesses. . . . It is high time that we restored decency to a major national sport. The corruption that is dominating the boxing profession . . . is not only a violation of our laws, but a violation of our democratic ideals." Engle, Kefauver, and other reform-minded congressmen hoped that a federal commission would do for boxing what Judge Landis had done for organized baseball following the Black Sox scandal.[34]

Engle preceded a panel of former boxing stars. Rocky Marciano claimed that it was "absolutely essential" that a federal czar for the sport be named. He envisioned the federal commission as a "policeman on the corner with a big stick." Moreover, Marciano proposed that the federal commission should serve as a "little FBI" and even suggested Frank Bonomi as a good choice for czar. Speaking in his "proper South Bostonian accent," Marciano seemed "as much at ease in the witness chair as if it were a ring stool," according to the *Washington Post*. Besides supporting the idea of a federal commission, he suggested other possible reforms for the sport, such as revised tax laws that would automatically remove a fighter's taxes from his purse and the development of some sort of minor leagues for professional boxing. In sum, Marciano impressed the subcommittee with his articulate statement and his strong support of the proposed legislation.[35]

Other former champions agreed with Marciano. Jack Dempsey and Gene Tunney gave back-to-back statements supporting the proposed federal commission. Age 66 and 64, respectively, the men spent more time answering questions about their illustrious careers than discussing the merits of the proposed legislation. But when given the opportunity, Dempsey claimed that a federal commission was the only thing that could save a sport "on its last legs."[36] (In a television interview a few weeks before the hearings, Dempsey had remarked, "control of boxing by hoodlums is sickening. . . . [The] fight game is about finished.")[37] Tunney concurred with Dempsey's analysis.[38]

Finally, the subcommittee listened to testimony from another great champ, Joe Louis. The "Brown Bomber" claimed that the criminal element had made boxing the "disgrace of all sports in America."[39] As for the bill, Louis "wholeheartedly" supported it, stating that he was "hoping and praying" that it would pass, as it would be the "best thing that ever happened to boxing."[40]

Other representatives from the sport agreed. Melvin Krulewitch, chairman of the New York State Athletic Commission, stated that, although he generally opposed federal intervention in matters of state regulation, boxing was a special case that did require federal intervention.[41] Harry Falk, member of the California Athletic Commission, agreed with Krulewitch. He explained that boxing was unlike the professional team sports in that it lacked the capacity to regulate itself. Without a federal commission, Falk predicted, the sport would continue to sink into monopoly.

Moreover, he pointed out that the sport lacked uniform codes, with rules varying from state to state. Falk surmised that a federal agency could correct the inconsistencies in state regulations and do for the sport what the state commissions could not. Falk concluded his testimony by telling the subcommittee that "everyone in the boxing world" not only supported this bill; they believed it was "absolutely essential to the preservation of boxing." No other industry, noted Falk, had ever come to Congress and admitted that it was "helpless" and in need of federal regulation.[42]

Other representatives from the sport joined in the chorus supporting the bill, including Nat S. Fleischer, president and editor of *Ring* magazine, and Alfred M. Klein, a member of the Pennsylvania Athletic Commission.[43] In a display rarely witnessed in congressional hearings, everyone associated with the professional sport supported the proposed legislation.

But for all of the support that the bill commanded in the congressional hearing room, it failed to reach the Senate floor for a vote. The primary reason for the bill's failure was disagreement between Congress and the Justice Department over the location of the proposed federal boxing commission. Kefauver's subcommittee believed that the best place for the commission was within the Justice Department because it could utilize the FBI as an investigative and enforcement tool.[44] However, Robert F. Kennedy, the recently appointed attorney general, disagreed with Kefauver and made it clear that he did not want the Justice Department to be saddled with a new regulatory commission.[45] Thus, despite the bill's overwhelming support within professional boxing and Congress, it never reached the Senate floor for a vote.

As the third round of congressional hearings came to a close, the boxing world was shaken by the news that Benny "Kid" Paret had died on April 3, 1962, after nine days in a coma following his welterweight bout with Emile Griffith. Paret's death was one of an estimated 174 boxing-related deaths between the years 1947 and 1960. Some commentators began to question the sport's value to society. The Vatican characterized the sport as "objectively immoral . . . brutal and demoralizing," comparing it to gladiatorial combat. Boxing, the Vatican continued, was "the most savage sport known to man since Nero and the lions." Others agreed. Facing a tough opponent named Richard M. Nixon in his reelection bid for the governorship of California, Governor Edmund G. Brown called the fight game "dirty, rotten, and brutalizing." His opponent concurred, arguing that the sport should be "cleaned up or kicked out, one or the other."[46] Political commentator David Brinkley observed that "many think boxing is an ugly brontosaurus that has somehow survived beyond its time." While he admitted that the sport did offer a route for a few young men to get out of the slums and into a "purple Cadillac," he noted that "the same is true of purse-snatching or pushing marijuana." As for the heavyweight champion, Brinkley declared that Sonny Liston is "the only fighter we know who's been arrested more times than he's fought."[47]

The sport's public image took a beating in the early 1960s. The game was certainly suffering from a lack of role models; it had a heavyweight champion who was an illiterate ex-convict and a challenger named Cassius Clay who reminded some more of Jack Johnson (for his volubility, if not his fighting talent) than Joe Louis. Brinkley characterized Clay (after he defeated Liston) as a "world champion in two divisions—heavyweight and loudmouth."[48] Aside from their public images, these leading heavyweights produced two controversial fights in 1964 and 1965, which led many observers again to question the integrity of the sport, and congressmen to call for renewed hearings on the matter of a federal boxing commission.

Round three of the congressional hearings on professional boxing proved to be Senator Kefauver's last, but just as he had done with professional team sports, Senator Philip Hart picked up the issue as chairman of the Senate Subcommittee on Anti-Trust and Monopoly. The fourth round of congressional hearings was called to investigate the controversy surrounding the first Liston-Clay fight, which took place on February 25, 1964, in Miami Beach, Florida. Clay won the fight and became the heavyweight champion, but only after a tired Sonny Liston refused to answer the bell for the eighth round. Liston claimed to be suffering from a sore left arm (an examination after the fight proved that he had torn a muscle).[49] But the facts that the pre-fight contract contained a "rematch clause" guaranteeing Liston a chance to reclaim his title should he lose it to Clay, and that several known underworld figures had spent a lot of time in Liston's camp, made some observers fear that the fight was not on the up and up. For that reason, Senator Hart revived the antitrust subcommittee's investigation into professional boxing during the last week of March 1964.

The subcommittee was willing to accept the report of Florida state's attorney, Richard E. Gerstein, which contained the results of the state's examination into the Liston-Clay fight. Gerstein's report cited the bona-fide injury to Liston's arm, but also noted the pre-fight rematch contract and the well-known assortment of underworld figures hanging around Liston's training camp. Despite those realities, the report concluded that there was insufficient evidence to prove the fight had been fixed.[50] Still, public confidence in the sport had been dealt a serious blow, and the subcommittee was interested in finding out whether "the same conditions that promoted the outpouring of support for the [Kefauver bill] exist today."[51]

The subcommittee heard testimony from representatives of Cassius Clay, now calling himself Muhammad Ali, and Sonny Liston. Gordon B. Davidson, attorney for the so-called Group of Eleven, the

Louisville businessmen who financially supported the boxing career of Cassius Clay, testified that the Clay camp was forced into signing the infamous rematch clause to get a title bout with Liston.[52] Davidson admitted that the Louisville group knew the World Boxing Association frowned on such clauses, but he claimed that their hands were tied.[53]

Senator Thruston B. Morton of Kentucky gave the subcommittee his personal endorsement of the Louisville group and claimed that they had the boxing game's best interests in mind.[54] Indeed, the Louisville group had set up a relationship with Cassius Clay that seemed more than fair. Under the arrangement, the young fighter did not have to hold a regular job, but received a salary for training full-time. Also, 15% of his earnings were put in a trust fund that he could not touch until he was either 35 years old or retired. Davidson characterized the arrangement as "the best deal a young fighter could have."[55] Indeed, contended Senator Morton, if more young fighters were as fortunate as Clay, the subcommittee hearings might not have been necessary.

One fighter who was clearly less fortunate in terms of management was Clay's opponent, Sonny Liston. Whereas the subcommittee was willing to take much of what Davidson said at face value, they were more wary where Liston's representatives were concerned. The subcommittee listened to testimony from Jack Nilon, Liston's manager at the Clay fight. Liston did not have a licensed manager at the time of the fight, but Nilon served the purpose for Liston who was, according to Nilon, a "neurotic, a hypochondriac, and a victim of overconfidence and superstition."[56] Nilon claimed that the champ refused to listen to his advice and trained too lightly for the match with Clay. Nilon had a definite interest in Liston's career, as he and his brother, Robert, had signed an exclusive deal with Liston giving their corporation, Intercontinental Promotions, the right to promote Liston's fights for six years. The deal had been struck in 1962, when Jack Nilon became Liston's unofficial manager following Senator Kefauver's warning to Liston to get rid of the criminal elements in his management.

Yet, criminal elements had clearly remained in Liston's corner; in fact Liston was introduced to the Nilon brothers by Sam Margolis, a friend and business associate of Blinky Palermo. Moreover, Margolis testified that Liston, as a gesture of gratitude for Margolis's having introduced him to the Nilon brothers, had signed over half of his stock in Intercontinental Promotions, worth $100,000.[57] In light of Liston's business savvy, the whole arrangement seemed more than suspicious to the subcommittee.

When asked by one senator if the Liston-Clay fight was fixed, however, Margolis replied "absolutely not."[58] As for the rematch clause, Robert Nilon testified that the clause was little more than an insurance policy; nobody in the Liston camp ever seriously believed that Clay would win the fight.[59] The subcommittee was hard pressed to find any evidence that the first Liston-Clay bout had been fixed; with the possible exception of Liston, probably no one could say for sure what happened the night of the fight. But the subcommittee felt confident that it had proved one thing: professional boxing was still heavily influenced by the underworld and a federal boxing commission could still be justified.

Many within the sport had not forgotten about Kefauver's boxing bill and had always maintained their support of it. In August 1963 Melvin Krulewitch wrote Senator Keating to remind him of Kefauver's bill and to urge its passage despite the death of the senator from Tennessee.[60] Senator Hart had also received dozens of letters from officials and fans in support of a federal boxing commission.[61] Also, shortly after the congressional hearings had concluded, another boxer died of injuries incurred within the ring. After undergoing three brain operations, heavyweight Alejandro Lavorante died of head injuries suffered during his 1962 bout with Johnny Riggins.

But despite Paret's and Lavorante's deaths, the subcommittee's clear evidence concerning the influence of criminals in the sport, and the support of nearly everyone within and without professional boxing, the boxing reform bill of 1964 never came close to passage. The bill faced the same difficulty in 1964 that it had faced three years earlier—failure to agree on the location of the proposed federal boxing commission. Again, legislators wanted to place it within the Justice Department; again, Attorney General Robert F. Kennedy absolutely refused.[62] Although Senator Hart even suggested that the commission might be placed in the Department of Commerce, the legislation failed to make headway in 1964.[63]

Still, boxing reformers were not completely shut out in 1964. On June 6, President Lyndon Johnson signed the Federal Sports Bribery Act. In February 1963 Senator Keating had introduced the bill that provided penalties of up to ten years in prison and $4,000 in fines for anyone caught fixing a sports contest.[64] Yet, as James H. Frey has pointed out, the law would not be enforced often enough to make much of a difference.[65] But in 1964, the Sports Bribery Law represented a small victory for those who wanted to reform professional boxing.

The fifth round of congressional hearings on professional boxing occurred the following year. The primary event that precipitated the 1965 hearing was the second Liston-Clay fight, held on May 25, 1965, in the small town of Lewiston, Maine. In what the weekly magazine *Time* characterized as the "theater of the absurd," Cassius Clay knocked out Sonny Liston during the first round of their highly publicized rematch. As *Time* described it, "[T]he bell for the first round had hardly sounded when Clay quickly banged a right off Liston's ear and went hippity-hopping around the ring. . . . Seconds later [he] flicked a right-hand chop that traveled no more than a foot to the side of Sonny's head. Liston sank to the canvas, rolled over onto his back, struggled to his knees, and went down again."[66]

The article stopped short of crying "fix," but others did not. Veteran boxing writer Jimmy Cannon claimed, "I was sitting right there. I saw the punch, and it couldn't have crushed a grape." Many, including Howard Cosell, one of Ali's few friends in the sports media, also had doubts about the honesty of the fight. He would later write, "If boxing can survive this, it can survive anything." Total pandemonium broke out at ringside following the fight, as students from nearby Bates College flooded the aisles yelling "FIX! FIX! FIX!"[67] Although *Sports Illustrated* published what were supposedly conclusive photographs proving that Ali had delivered a "perfectly valid, stunning right-hand punch," many public officials argued that the sport's integrity was beyond redemption.[68] State laws were introduced in Pennsylvania and New York to ban the sport; in Washington, D.C., members of Congress again seized the opportunity to commence hearings on professional boxing.[69]

The 1965 hearings differed from previous hearings in that they were held in the House rather than the Senate. In July the House held hearings on the formation of a federal boxing commission that would have the power to prevent the televising or broadcasting of any bout it deemed affected in any way by bribery, collusion, or racketeering. The bill, H.R. 8635, was introduced by Arkansas Representative Oren Harris on May 27, in the aftermath of the Liston-Clay fight. Unlike previous Senate bills, the Harris bill did not give the federal boxing commission the right to license or the power to force disclosure of fight contracts.[70] Rather, the Harris bill was concerned with insuring "that channels of interstate commerce are free from false or fraudulent descriptions or depictions of professional boxing contests."[71] The air waves were important because while Liston-Clay II made only $200,000 at the gate, it cleared an additional $4 million in closed-circuit revenues.[72] And House members generally concurred with Emanuel Celler, who remarked, "I pity the suckers who paid $40 [or] $50 for seats in various theaters throughout the country for half a minute's fiasco."[73]

The U.S. House of Representatives Committee on Interstate and Foreign Commerce gathered to hear testimony from leading figures within professional boxing on the merits of the Harris bill. On July 6, a trio of former champions again lent their full support for the bill before a standing-room-only crowd.[74] Jack Dempsey testified that the sport had "deteriorated" and that it was "high time" for something to be done.[75] Gene Tunney also "strongly" supported the bill, claiming that if Congress had acted sooner, the country would have been saved the four recent "sorry spectacles" in the heavyweight division (including Liston's two easy knockouts of Floyd Patterson), and would not have been "bilked out" of $30 million in live gate and closed-circuit television revenues.[76]

Finally, Rocky Marciano testified that "boxing is in such a bad position" because "devious and unwholesome" elements controlled the sport. As Dempsey and Tunney had done before him, Marciano fully supported the concept of a federal boxing commission, but went on to suggest that the Harris bill did not go far enough because it failed to provide the proposed commission with licensing powers. In general, though, the three champions had great faith that the "Federals" could solve boxing's ills.[77]

As in previous congressional inquiries, a long procession of other prominent figures testified in favor of a federal commission. Nat Fleischer of *Ring* felt that the sport needed a "National Commissioner with regulatory powers with teeth that give him an iron hand in control of boxing." Furthermore, he suggested, such a regulatory body could create national rules for the sport in place of varying state regulations.[78] Melvin Krulewitch claimed that the bill was a "shot in the right direction," although it failed to "hit the bulls-eye" because it did not go far enough. Like Marciano, Krulewitch believed that, to be effective, a federal commission needed to have general licensing power in addition to regulatory powers over the broadcasts and telecasts of fights.[79] Finally, Arch Hindman, executive secretary of the World Boxing Association, "heartily" endorsed the bill and admitted that professional boxing needed "Uncle Sam's help." He agreed with Marciano and Krulewitch, however, that the Harris bill probably did not go far enough in its regulatory powers.[80]

Only one of seventeen witnesses spoke out against the bill. William Reitzer, who described himself as a Washington writer and special investigator, opposed a federal boxing commission on the grounds that the sport needed to be abolished on account of its brutality.[81] Representative Torbert H. MacDonald of Massachusetts also voiced reservations about the bill. He felt that "too much" had been "made out of it." MacDonald added that "there are, after all, other things that could be corrected in the affairs of this nation" which should "take priority" over professional boxing.[82] But these reservations concerning the bill were faint cries in a loud cheer of support.

The support for the Harris bill carried it to the floor of the House, where it passed overwhelmingly, 346 to 4, on August 16.[83] In its House-passed form, the Harris bill provided for a three-man federal boxing commission with the power to pull the broadcasting plug on any fight it suspected of being influenced by bribery or racketeering. Also, the subcommittee heeded the advice of its witnesses and gave the commission general licensing power over managers, promoters, matchmakers, and fighters. Members of the commission were to be appointed by the President and serve six-year terms. Finally, violators faced penalties of up to five years in prison and/or $50,000 in fines.[84]

The passage of the Harris bill gave Senator Hart renewed confidence that his bill could pass the Senate. The Hart bill differed slightly from the Harris bill in that it called for a single commissioner rather than a commission, and it placed the commissioner under the auspices of the Justice Department. The Harris bill left the placement of its commission up to question. Hart believed that his bill would pass the Senate by Thanksgiving and that a joint committee could work out a compromise bill for the President to sign shortly thereafter. But Hart's enthusiasm was ill-founded; his bill never reached the Senate for a vote.[85]

Thus, Congress adjourned in 1965 without having created a federal boxing commission. The passage of the Harris bill in the House would be the closest that professional boxing had ever come to outright federal regulation.

Congress waited until the late 1970s before again considering the creation of a federal boxing commission. The sixth round of congressional hearings had to do with a bill called the Federal Boxing Control Act, introduced in the spring of 1979 by Representative Edward P. Beard of Rhode Island, chairman of the House Subcommittee on Labor Standards. Beard, who had had a short career as a professional boxer in the late 1950s, claimed that the sport was being controlled by a few powerful promoters. The Beard bill sought to create a three-man federal boxing board within the Department of Labor. The board would have general regulatory powers, including the power to license managers, promoters, and fighters, as well as set health standards for the sport.[86]

Beard's subcommittee heard testimony from representatives of professional boxing on March 28–29 and April 3. Floyd Patterson, former heavyweight champion and current member of the New York State Athletic Commission, testified in support of Beard's bill. Patterson claimed that the unanimous opinion of the NYSAC was that the sport needed some type of federal regulatory agency. He added that the primary justification for such a body was the need to correct the inconsistent rules of the various state athletic commissions.[87]

Howard Cosell also testified on behalf of the bill. He believed that a federal commission would "eliminate, generally, the chaos of the sport and it would establish clout that would have to be recognized by the current rump organizations, the WBA and the WBC." Cosell cited the inequities in international ratings systems, inconsistent health standards and rules, and the fiasco of having several heavyweight champions as justifications for the creation of a federal commission.[88] (In the late 1960s and early 1970s the governance of the sport had splintered between the World Boxing Council, the World Boxing Association, and the International Boxing Federation.)

Unlike the hearings of the early 1960s, those of 1979 included considerable testimony in opposition to the idea of a federal commission. Jersey Joe Walcott protested that the bill made a "whipping boy" out of the sport. Walcott described boxing as "the greatest sport in the world," and went on to declare that during his career he was neither offered a bribe nor knew of any corruption within the sport. Walcott also charged that the congressmen were meddling in a sport about which they knew little. When Chairman Beard informed Walcott that he had done "a little boxing" before becoming a congressman, Walcott responded by saying, "that's the trouble, you did a 'little' boxing."[89]

Don King, one of the game's most controversial promoters, also testified in opposition to the bill. Like Walcott, King argued that Congress was unfairly singling out professional boxing; if a federal boxing commission was needed, then a general federal sports commission should be created as well. Otherwise, he stated, boxing's image would be damaged rather than rehabilitated; the game would look like the "little black ugly duckling . . . of the sports field." King believed that a better course of action would be to upgrade the state commissions. But he added in conclusion, "If I were to rank, in order of importance, problems requiring the attention of the federal government, surely professional sports . . . would rank very close to the bottom of the list."[90] As the hearings drew to a close, Chairman Beard said that he would not work for passage of his bill until the following year, but 1980 also passed without the Beard bill's even reaching the floor of the House.

The seventh round of congressional hearings on professional boxing took place in the winter of 1983. The House Subcommittee on Commerce, Transportation, and Tourism, chaired by Representative James Florio of New Jersey, held hearings on the proposed Congressional Advisory Commission on Boxing Act. The bill aimed to create a special congressional commission with powers to investigate the sport and make legislative suggestions to Congress, serving a purpose similar to that of the 1976 Select Committee on Sports. Florio's bill was prompted, in large part, by the 1982 death of Korean middleweight contender Duk Koo Kim, who died of head injuries sustained in a fight with Ray "Boom Boom" Mancini.

Florio's subcommittee listened to a number of witnesses who strongly supported Florio's bill. Floyd Patterson again testified in favor of a federal boxing commission. He believed that such a commission could standardize safety rules and cut down on the number of serious injuries within the sport. Patterson suggested that the sport adopt a thumbless glove to end the type of eye injury that had recently sent "Sugar Ray" Leonard into (temporary) retirement. The answer to boxing's ills, according to Patterson, was a federal commission that could do the things state commissions could not. Patterson concluded by pleading with Congress to refrain from considering the abolition of the sport. He believed that boxing served a useful purpose in society as an avenue for kids to escape the "ghettos."[91]

Howard Cosell was not at all upbeat about boxing's place in American society. The ABC sportscaster had recently said that he would no longer cover boxing for his network because of the sport's brutality. Cosell made his announcement following a heavyweight title match involving champion Larry Holmes and challenger Tex Cobb. During that fight, which Holmes easily won, Cobb endured 26 unanswered blows. The experience proved too much for Cosell to stomach. He testified that the sport was "desperately sick," and that a federal boxing commission was the game's only hope. Minus a federal commission, Cosell suggested that prizefighting might need to be abolished. Sweden and Norway, he pointed out, had abolished professional boxing, "and there has been no noticeable deterioration in their respective civilizations."

An increasing number of observers agreed with Cosell. Dr. George Lundberg, editor of the *Journal of the American Medical Association*, called for either more rigorous safety standards or the total abolition of boxing.[92] Finally, Cosell told the subcommittee that the sport was still monopolistic as well as dangerous, charging that promoter Don King controlled the heavyweight division in the same way that the IBC had controlled it in the early 1960s.[93]

Other witnesses also supported the bill. Donald Fraser, executive director of the California State Athletic Commission, believed that a federal commission would be especially helpful in keeping accurate records of fighters' health records.[94] Bert Sugar, successor to Nat Fleischer as publisher of *Ring* magazine, agreed with Fraser; the World Boxing Council and the World Boxing Association were doing an inadequate job regulating the sport. The WBA, for example, had Duk Koo Kim ranked as the number one contender for Mancini's crown, but according to *Ring*, Kim was not among the top 40 contenders for the championship. Sugar suggested that a more uniform ranking system could avoid such mismatches in the future. Although Sugar was somewhat skeptical about how effective a powerful national commission would be, he did feel that a commission exercising general oversight powers and leaving a lot of authority at the state level could be extremely important to boxing's survival.[95]

Unlike congressional witnesses in 1979, the witnesses before the Florio subcommittee unanimously supported the concept of federal intervention into professional boxing. Although the Committee on Energy and Commerce favorably reported the bill to the floor of the

House, the measure was defeated on July 26, 1983, by a vote of 254 to 167.[96] Thus, like earlier congressional inquiries, the seventh round on professional boxing produced no legislation.

* * *

Despite hearings, nearly unanimous support within the sport of boxing, and clear evidence of criminal and monopolistic influences, Congress failed to create a federal boxing commission. On one hand there are clear bureaucratic explanations for this failure, the foremost being the inability of officials within the legislative and executive branches of the federal government to agree on where such a boxing commission should be located. Congressmen generally wanted to place it in the Justice Department to give it access to the FBI, but Attorney General Kennedy thwarted these attempts in the early 1960s because he did not want his department to be strapped with the responsibility of overseeing professional boxing. While subsequent efforts were made to set up a federal boxing commission within the Department of Commerce, these efforts were generally weak and never came close to producing desired results. Thus, an interesting jurisdictional dispute was one factor that stymied the creation of a federal boxing commission.

On the other hand, Congress's failure to create a national boxing commission can be explained by the public image of the sport. Boxing has always struggled to maintain a healthy public image. Such an image was at its peak in the 1920s and 1930s, but in the post-World War II era the sport has had an image of being only one step ahead of the law. Over the last 40 years the fight game has been represented, in part, by notorious figures such as Frankie Carbo, Blinky Palermo, James Norris, and Don King, and by athletes such as Sonny Liston and Mike Tyson. Ring deaths, serious injuries, and the exploitation of young, poor, uneducated (often black) males were additional spots on the sport's character. In 1965 a Gallup poll revealed that 42% of the American public believed the sport should be abolished.[97] To be sure, the sport has always kept its share of die-hard fans, but it is also likely that at no time did 42% of Americans feel that organized baseball deserved abolition.

Just as organized baseball's image as the patriotic, pastoral, and innocent national pastime paralyzed legislative attempts to place it under the antitrust laws, boxing's image as the "red light district" of professional sports thwarted congressional efforts to place it under a federal regulatory commission.[98] The creation of a federal boxing commission might indirectly give the sport a legitimacy and importance that many Americans do not feel it deserves. After all, each of the professional sports had faced crises over the years, but they had found ways to deal with them without the permanent assistance of the federal government.

Too, a federal boxing commission could not be had for free; such an agency would cost money. It would also clearly break precedent as Congress has never allocated public monies for the purpose of regulating or supporting professional sports (aside from the resources spent on hearings and investigations). If the government could not justify spending tax dollars regulating or supporting professional baseball or professional football, certainly it could not spend tax dollars to save the "red-light district" of professional sports. Thus, the fight game found itself in a Catch-22 position. Boxing pleaded for congressional help to upgrade and maintain its integrity, but the widespread perception that the sport lacked honesty and integrity was the very thing that kept Congress from granting boxing what it desired.

Therefore, as in the case of professional baseball and the antitrust laws, much of the explanation for Congress's treatment of professional boxing lies in the public image projected by the sport. In sum, what congressman could justify spending taxpayer dollars and governmental resources on a sport that many voters believed ought to be abolished?

Part II

Congress and Professional Sports Broadcasting

Chapter 6

Eating Their Young, 1953–61

Congress's first attention to the issue of professional sports broadcasting resulted from growing tension in the early 1950s having to do with telecasts of major league and minor league baseball teams. While minor league ball had flourished in the early post-war years, by the mid-1950s the minors increasingly found themselves in financial distress. The minors attracted some 42 million fans in 1949, but by 1957 attendance at minor league games had fallen to 15 million.[1] With a decline in attendance came the collapse of numerous minor leagues. Whereas 59 minor leagues operated in 1949, by 1953—the time of the first congressional hearing on baseball broadcasting policies—only 39 minor league teams remained solvent, In Ohio the number of minor leagues teams dropped from 17 to 2 during the same period.[2]

Observers of the game debated the causes for the difficulties of the minors. One factor was that by the 1950s Americans enjoyed a wider variety of leisure activities; for example, so-called participation sports, such as golf, tennis, and bowling, were increasingly accessible. Moreover, in this period Americans also had a greater assortment of material goods on which to spend their money. Some also suggested that the minors' decline was caused by the fact that organized baseball strictly forbade gambling; money spent at horse-racing tracks increased during the decade.[3]

All of these factors contributed to the decline in minor league baseball in the middle and late 1950s, but many believed that the primary culprits in the minors' collapse were the U.S. Justice Department and the major leagues. In fact, the major leagues also suffered a decline in attendance, particularly in the early 1950s, but they did not experience such devastating drops as the minors. Improved transportation was one reason; more and more fans owned automobiles and drove them a considerable distance to see major league teams play. However, the shift in attendance was also caused by changes in the game's broadcasting policies resulting from pressure by the Justice Department.

85

Beginning in 1941, organized baseball operated under a broadcasting system that protected "home territories" from outside telecasts. The system was codified under Commissioner Kenesaw Mountain Landis's tenure in rule 1(d), which stated that no ball club could broadcast its games into the home territory of another club, major or minor, without the permission of the home team. The rationale for the policy was simple; Landis believed that it was necessary to keep stronger teams from robbing weaker ones of their broadcast markets. But by 1951, rule 1(d) came under heavy fire from the Justice Department because of its monopolistic features; a half dozen law suits were filed against organized baseball. Although the game stood pat initially, by the end of the year the owners repealed rule 1(d) in the face of litigation.[4] Thus by the mid-1950s, rather than pay to see a local minor league team on a given Saturday, many could watch big league ball in the comfort of their living rooms for free.

Officials within the game had argued that the elimination of rule 1(d) would destroy the minors, and by 1953 their fears seemed justified. One of these officials was Edwin C. Johnson, president of the Western League. Johnson, aside from serving as head of a struggling class A circuit, also worked as a Democratic U.S. senator from Colorado. Senator Johnson decided to use his influence on Capitol Hill to bring help to the ailing minor leagues. He attempted to do so in 1953 and 1954 through the introduction of bills into the Senate. The bills and the hearings they spawned were quite different in content, but they were both introduced for the same purpose—relief for the minor leagues.

The first of Johnson's bills was S. 1396, a piece of "permissive legislation" designed to "stop the trend of the destruction of minor league baseball and forestall the liquidation of the sport itself."[5] Essentially, the bill was drafted to legislate an exemption for rule 1(d) and thereby "protect the weak and helpless elements of America's national game of baseball." Senator Johnson argued that the game had become the victim of an overzealous Justice Department, which, despite "good faith and the purest of intentions," had "struck a foul blow against America's great grassroots sport."[6] An interesting characteristic of S. 1396, however, was that it would not have mandated organized baseball to reinstate rule 1(d) but only granted the sport permission to do so.

In May 1953 the Senate Committee on Interstate and Foreign Commerce held hearings to discuss baseball's dilemma and Johnson's legislative solution. A number of important witnesses testified at the hearings, with the majority heartily supporting Johnson's bill. Commissioner Ford Frick was one of them. Frick argued that while rule 1(d) was monopolistic by nature, the policy was essential to the survival of the sport. "If we had rugged individualism in our operation of baseball, baseball wouldn't exist 10 years," he claimed.[7] Frick also expressed concern about the possible effects of unlimited broadcasting, which he believed would ultimately be "harmful" and "detrimental" to the sport. Finally, he warned that a monopoly of a different kind might develop, wherein the richest and most successful teams would dominate the air waves.[8]

Other witnesses generally agreed with Commissioner Frick. George Trautman, president of the National Association of Baseball Leagues (the minors' overall governing body), declared that the minor leagues' problems were caused by the saturation of their broadcast markets by major league teams. He admitted that major league telecasts were not the only reason for the decline in minor league attendance, but he argued that they were the main culprit.[9] Warren C. Giles, National League president, concurred with Trautman's analysis concerning the invasion of minor league territories by the majors and fully supported Johnson's bill.[10]

Former baseball Commissioner A.B. "Happy" Chandler, one of the last witnesses to testify, also spoke in favor of S. 1396. Chandler argued that rule 1(d) was legal and pointed to the fact that it had never actually been declared otherwise by any court. He believed that the game should be allowed to determine the rule's merit without help by the Justice Department. Chandler continued, "the ideal system, of course, would be if every little community in the country owned its own ball club and was absolutely independent and free." Yet, he admitted that the nation was becoming oversaturated with baseball broadcasts, and that fans would not pay to see minor league games if they could watch major league games for free on television.[11] In sum, Chandler argued that rule 1(d) was necessary in order to keep major league teams from "eating their young" and ultimately destroying the game.

For all of the support it garnered, Johnson's bill also attracted some opposition. The most outspoken dissenter was Gordon McLendon, former head of the defunct Liberty Broadcasting Company. Liberty, comprised of more than 430 stations, had "re-created" major league games through teletype during 1948–51. In

1952, however, six teams asserted that they would not allow their games to be re-created and a Chicago federal court approved their assertion. Thus, Liberty Broadcasting had to shut down its operations. At the time of the hearings, McLendon was in the process of suing thirteen major league teams for monopolistic practices that had allegedly led to the fall of the Liberty network.[12]

McLendon opposed Johnson's bill on the grounds that it would deprive the American public of the right to see major league games. Instead of eating their young, McLendon believed, the majors were asking for the right to "eat the American public," which would be, he predicted, "a bit more difficult to digest." He warned that if Congress passed the bill, it would find its desks overflowing with "complaints from the broadcasting industry and the people. . . . It's a discriminatory bill and your constituents will be mad." Essentially, McLendon argued that a few of baseball's top owners were power-hungry, and that unrestricted broadcasts were in the interest of the public. McLendon concluded by insisting that the bill sought to give minor leagues a monopoly; the antitrust laws should not be laid aside for the protection of minor league baseball.[13]

Senator Johnson characterized McLendon as a "most provocative witness with a peculiar and selfish attitude," and labeled his testimony a "far-fetched" filibuster.[14] Part of the reason that McLendon received a less-than-sympathetic hearing from the subcommittee was that his network had been involved in recreations of major league games, a practice that Johnson described as a "fraud on the public.[15]

As the hearings drew to a close, Senator Johnson predicted an early passage for his bill.[16] The committee reported the bill favorably to the floor of the Senate, but when it came up for a vote on July 8, the Senate failed to approve it, despite the nearly unanimous support that the bill had in the hearing room and Senator Johnson's tireless efforts.[17] The Western League president warned his Senate colleagues that, like Humpty Dumpty, organized baseball was about to fall, and when it did, Congress might not be able to put it back together again.[18]

Senator Johnson continued his attempts to save the drowning minor leagues in the next session of Congress. In 1954 he introduced legislation designed to apply the antitrust laws to any ball club owned and operated by a member of the alcoholic beverage industry. The bill, S.J. 133, targeted the National League's St. Louis Cardinals; in fact, the proposal quickly became known as the "Anti-Cardinal bill."[19] Johnson focused his wrath upon Cardinals owner August A. Busch, because the franchise had taken advantage of the repeal of rule 1(d); Busch did not hesitate to broadcast Cardinals games into the territories of numerous minor league teams. In 1953, cities throughout the Midwest, including Columbus, Ohio; Houston, Texas; Wichita, Kansas; Omaha, Nebraska; and Indianapolis, Indiana, received coverage of Cardinals games despite the fact that each of these cities had a minor league franchise.[20] (Omaha and Wichita belonged to Johnson's Western League.) Senator Johnson determined, through the use of the antitrust laws, to coerce the St. Louis Cardinals owner into changing his club's broadcast policies.

As the hearings opened, however, it became clear that Johnson was fighting a lonesome battle. The Western League's president opened the hearings by claiming that an "unholy alliance" had been struck between the organized baseball and the alcohol industry. Baseball, he argued, sacrificed its antitrust exemption when it became so deeply involved with an industry that was clearly under the anti-trust laws. Johnson, like many other fans, was particularly disturbed by the fact that breweries had long enjoyed a foothold in the sport; at present, besides Anheuser-Busch's interest in the Cardinals, the Miller Brewing Company was interested in buying the Milwaukee Braves, according to reports. The senator from Colorado pointed out that Busch was able to use his ball club as a free advertising tool, which Johnson clearly believed was unethical if not illegal. All of this, though, was peripheral to the Cardinals' practice of broadcasting their games into the home territories of minor league teams. If the Cards had refrained from doing that, the 1954 hearings would not have been held.

Yet as the witnesses passed before the Senate Subcommittee on Anti-Trust and Monopoly, Johnson's hopes for his bill faded. One by one, they opposed S.J. 133 on the ground that it was unjust and discriminatory. Commissioner Frick testified that while the game's "chief headache" was the broadcasting issue and the demise of the minor leagues, Johnson's latest bill was not the appropriate pill for the game's pain.[21]

Assistant U.S. Attorney General Stanley W. Barnes agreed with Commissioner Frick's assessment of the "Anti-Cardinal bill." Barnes testified that the Justice Department opposed the legislation because it was "discriminatory" and did not treat baseball fairly. He added that although his department believed that baseball belonged under the antitrust laws, the Johnson bill was inadequate because it sought to apply the antitrust laws unevenly and would be too difficult to enforce. Barnes concluded that total application of the antitrust laws was the best solution, but a piecemeal application, such as provided in Johnson's bill, would be worse than complete exemption.[22]

Aside from Frick and Barnes, the subcommittee also listened to testimony from Joe Garagiola, radio announcer for the Cardinals. The subcommittee called Garagiola because rumors had circulated that the Cardinals had "tampered" with him by offering him a position in the Cardinals organization as a broadcaster while he was under contract as a player for the Chicago White Sox. Hoping to find a smoking gun that would implicate Busch's franchise, Johnson asked Garagiola about his relations with the Cardinals during the time he played for the White Sox. The witness frustrated but also amused the Colorado senator when he responded, "Tampering with me? Why I'm a .250 hitter, I was trying to get my own broadcasting job." In fact, the Cardinals had offered Garagiola a contract and he had joined the organization the previous winter as a broadcaster; but, according to him, the entire deal was carried out properly and without any contract tampering.[23]

The final witness to testify in 1954 was August A. Busch, the owner of the Cardinals and Anheuser-Busch breweries. Surprisingly, Busch's appearance before the subcommittee proved to be a pleasant one. The St. Louis "beer baron" defended himself against Senator Johnson's charge that he was "bent for minor league destruction through radio broadcasts," informing the subcommittee that the Cardinals had signed working agreements with five new minor league teams and had revived one that had not played at all the previous season.

As for the charge that he had purchased the ball club for its potential for free advertising, Busch testified that he bought the team the previous year solely to keep the franchise from relocating. He claimed that he would sell it to anyone who had the financing and the desire to keep the team in St. Louis. Moreover, Busch was remarkably forthcoming regarding the financial relationship between his ball club and his brewery, and generally convinced the subcommittee that his operations were above reproach.[24] One member of the subcommittee told Busch that he was "one of the best witnesses ever to appear before this committee . . . it makes me feel good to meet an American like you."[25]

As the hearings wrapped up, the subcommittee appeared sympathetic with neither Johnson nor his bill. Senator Everett Dirksen of Illinois declared that he would "move heaven and earth" to defeat Johnson's resolution. "I think my good friend sees dangers, phantoms under the bed, that are not there," said Dirksen.[26] The senator from Illinois claimed responsibility for the defeat of Johnson's 1953 bill, and he promised the same outcome for Johnson's 1954 offering. But Dirksen soon realized that he would not have to work as hard on that particular matter in 1954 as he had the previous year. The day after the hearings concluded, Senator Johnson announced that he was terminating his efforts to get S.J. 133 written into law.[27]

As for the Cardinals, the team announced during the hearings that in the future it would ask permission of minor league teams before sending broadcasts into their home territories.[28] But following 1954, neither the Cardinals nor any other major league franchise respected the territorial rights of minor league teams. Instead, major league teams continued to feed their broadcasts and telecasts into the territories of minor league teams; as a result, minor league attendance dropped to eleven million by 1973 and the number of minor leagues in operation fell to eighteen during the same period.[29] In fact, there is little evidence to suggest that rule 1(d) would have been respected by big-league owners even if organized baseball had been free to reinstate it.

The reality was that by the mid-1950s major league owners and the public felt that violations of minor league territories were justified.[30] Beginning in the summer of 1953, the American Broadcasting Company televised its *Game of the Week*. (The Columbia Broadcasting System took over the major league *Game of the Week* in 1955.) Although ABC's weekly games were blacked out around major league cities, minor league territories, particularly in the South and West, were invaded every Saturday afternoon. Curiously, while Johnson enthusiastically pursued Cardinals broadcasts, he failed to go after the network *Game of the Week* with equal fervor. Be that as it may, Johnson's failed attempts in 1953 and 1954 to create legislative salvation for the minor leagues proved to be Congress's last effort to deal directly with the demise of the minors and organized baseball's broadcasting policies.

The issue of professional sports broadcasting did not surface in Congress again until 1961, when the House Judiciary Committee held hearings on H.R. 8757, a bill to enable professional sports teams to pool their separate television rights and to sell the resulting package to a single television network. The purpose of this bill was to clear up what had become a foggy situation in professional sports broadcasting.

In July 1961, Federal District Judge Alan K. Grim handed down a ruling that invalidated a two-year contract between the National Football League and the Columbia Broadcasting System. The NFL had concerns about the legality of the contract and had submitted it to Judge Grim for a ruling. The contract was for a record $9.1 million and included 98 games; each team relinquished its own rights to sell to another network, enabling the league to act as a whole. Judge Grim stated that the contract went too far in eliminating competition between individual teams and violated the antitrust laws.[31] The fact that the National Basketball Association and the American Football League had been operating under similar contracts further complicated matters.

Thus, on August 28, 1961, the Judiciary Committee's Subcommittee on Anti-Trust and Monopoly convened to clear muddy waters. Chairman Emanuel Celler sponsored the House bill; a sister bill was proposed in the Senate by Celler's counterpart, Estes Kefauver.[32] The introduction of bills so friendly to professional sports seemed a bit out of character for "Congress's two chief trust-busters," but both men felt that Judge Grim's decision had been "unduly harsh."[33] Celler was also careful to point out that, if the Grim decision stood, the National Basketball Association and the American Football League, the National Football League's rival, would be in danger. For while the NFL might survive without the "package" contract, its rival could not.[34] The bills proposed by Celler and Kefauver appeared more in character in this light. In any case, the NFL was eager to have the matter decided as quickly as possible, and it looked as though Congress was willing to oblige.

The hearings lasted only one day and produced only a handful of witnesses. The most important was Alvin "Pete" Rozelle, the new commissioner of the NFL. Rozelle had taken over the position in 1959 after Bert Bell died. Trained in advertising, he had quickly won the respect of NFL owners as a shrewd businessman capable of lobbying for the interests of the league.[35]

Rozelle told the subcommittee that there were several teams in the league that were suffering financially because they were unable to cut the profitable deals with television networks that teams located in wealthier television markets were able to obtain. For example, in 1960 the Western Division champion Green Bay Packers collected about $75,000 for their radio-TV rights, but the Pittsburgh Steelers, an also-ran in the Eastern Division, garnered more than $225,000 for their rights.[36] Teams in New York and Washington, D.C., collected even more broadcast revenues. According to Rozelle, besides Green Bay, the Detroit, Dallas, and Minneapolis franchises were struggling to keep up with teams in the larger markets.[37] In short, Rozelle relied on the "league" concept; that is, a league cannot withstand open competition among its teams for broadcasting rights. The result would be, Rozelle predicted, a growing number of "sick" clubs as the "rich get richer and the poor get poorer."[38]

The majority of witnesses favored the bill, including Ford Frick. Frick pointed out, though, that the bill did not really affect organized baseball, as each of its member teams received most of its television revenues from independent contracts with regional television networks.[39] A few witnesses opposed the legislation, however, including Vincent T. Wasilewski, vice-president of government affairs for the National Association of Broadcasters. He said the bill would give the NFL a "blank check" to determine which games could and could not be telecast. Wasilewski also pointed out that if a network gained exclusive control over one league, the "possibility of two networks telecasting different games of the same league in the same area" would be eliminated.[40]

Those in the broadcasting industry who opposed the legislation did so for basically the same reasons that they opposed the 1953 legislation. But their "open competition" arguments were no more appealing this time around. Along with the National Association of Broadcasters, the Justice Department stated publicly that it opposed the Celler-Kefauver bills. The department feared that the legislation would grant professional sports leagues an exemption that might be used to cover more than simply package-broadcasting deals.[41] As for the major networks, they remained uncharacteristically silent throughout the process. One writer has suggested that they did not want to anger the professional sports leagues by opposing the bills, and they realized that opposition was futile in any case.[42]

Ultimately, opposition did prove futile; both houses of Congress passed the Sports Broadcasting Act of 1961 and President John F. Kennedy signed the bill into law.[43] The NFL lobbied Congress so effectively that the bill was passed within two months of its introduction.[44] The results of Congress's actions were felt almost immediately. Of course, the law benefited professional football, as teams such as the Green Bay Packers, who had a viewing audience of 63,000, could collect the same television profit as the New York Giants, who had a viewing audience of more than 8 million. Soon both the NFL and AFL would sign package contracts worth record amounts with the CBS and NBC networks, respectively.

But a more equal distribution of television profits was not the only result of the 1961 legislation. Another important outcome was the protection that the law granted to college football. A peripheral issue debated during the hearings was the possibility of professional football's edging out college football in the race for television time. Thus, a section was added to the bill denying exemption for any package contract that allowed the televising of professional games after 6:00 P.M.. on Fridays or on Saturdays, beginning on the second Friday in September and ending on the second Saturday in December.[45]

Essentially, Congress granted the protection to college football in 1961 that it failed to grant minor league baseball in 1953. In light of the fact that college football has become a multi-million dollar enterprise, largely because of its Saturday afternoon broadcasts, it is interesting to speculate on what might have become of college football had this protection not been granted. During his testimony, Rozelle worked hard to convince the subcommittee that the NFL planned to respect the time traditionally and voluntarily allotted to college ball.[46] Yet, there is evidence that while the NFL lobbied for passage of the bill, it also lobbied for the removal of the section that granted protection to college football.[47]

Clearly, the professional game wanted to retain the freedom to broadcast its games on Saturday afternoons and evenings. Although the league's efforts in this direction failed, Congress acted swiftly in the late summer of 1961 to grant professional football an antitrust exemption for its package broadcasting contracts. Ironically, this exemption, and another granted in 1966 for the NFL-AFL merger, would haunt professional football when it became engaged in a bitter fight with Congress over its long-standing practice of blacking out home games.

Chapter 7

The Forty-Thousand-Dollar Quarterback, 1962–92

The Sports Broadcasting Act of 1961 was probably the most important facilitator in the rise of professional football in the late 1960s and early 1970s. The sport was perfectly suited to the medium of television, and networks were willing to pay unheard-of sums of money for the rights to broadcast professional football games.[1] In 1964 the NFL signed a whopping $28.2 million deal with CBS for two seasons.[2] As a result, each team in the league was guaranteed $1 million in television revenues over the next two seasons. The AFL also cashed in through a package contract it obtained with NBC worth $42 million over five years; each AFL team was assured $850,000 per season in television revenues.[3] In 1966, the AFL would provide such stiff competition to the NFL that the two would effect a merger, a peripheral result of the 1961 exemption that "Congress's chief trustbusters" failed to anticipate. Through package agreements and a merger, football rose to dominate the professional sports world. Yet, domination and popularity brought public pressure to bear on one of the game's long-held broadcasting policies—the blackout rule.

Professional football had been blacking out televised games in the home team's territory since 1953, when Federal District Court Judge Alan K. Grim granted it the right to do so.[4] Judge Grim ruled that such a policy was reasonable because it would facilitate higher gate revenues, vital to the league's existence before the advent of package contracts. But as professional football and television enjoyed the benefits of their deal, fans became increasingly impatient and irritated by the league's blackout policy. Many sought ways to circumvent the rule. For example, in the early 1960s the Stratford Motor Inn, in Stratford, Connecticut, gained a name for itself as a provider of bootleg TV. With its 50-foot antenna, the motel could receive a signal from Hartford carrying New York Giants games. Thus, for Giants fans willing to drive to Stratford, a "big, beautiful private room, a 21-inch television set . . . [and] plenty of glasses and ice" could be reserved for $10.35, though there was a limit of four to a room. The manager of the Stratford Inn claimed that he made $10,000 as a result of the NFL's blackout policy.

The Stratford Inn was not the only motel to take advantage of the situation. Some were bold enough to advertise rooms in local papers for the purpose of viewing blacked out games.[5] These Sunday afternoon sojourns grew tiresome, however, and by the early 1970s many fans and some congressmen began questioning the necessity of the NFL's blackout policy.

The blackout controversy lasted for most of a decade and was not only drawn out but also complicated. Nevertheless, the story can be neatly divided into three phases. The first phase, which lasted from fall 1972 to fall 1973, contained the vain initial struggle of the NFL to head off the antiblackout legislation before it snowballed its way through Congress. The legislation that passed in 1973 was temporary, not to be made permanent until its full effect could be gauged. The second phase, lasting from fall 1973 to winter 1975, was the trial period for the bill. The Federal Communications Commission monitored the law to determine its validity and usefulness to the public. The third phase started at the beginning of 1976, when Congress failed to make the law permanent, and sputtered through the second half of the decade.

On October 10, 1972, the *New York Times* printed a story stating that President Richard Nixon had thrown his complete support behind a new sports bill pending in Congress. The bill was S. 4007 or, simply, the antiblackout bill, and it was sponsored by Senator Robert Griffin of Michigan and later by Senator John O. Pastore of Rhode Island. By the early 1970s, tickets for many NFL home games were difficult, if not impossible, for the average fan to obtain because of the high number of season-ticket holders and early sellouts. Therefore, many fans, including President Nixon—"the nation's number one football fan"—became impatient with the National Football League's blackout policy, viewing it as unnecessary and unfair to the loyal fan. Nixon even declared that he expected Congress to have the legislation on his desk before it adjourned in mid-October.[6] With the clear support of the White House and football fans, Congress moved quickly to call hearings on the antiblackout measure.

The first hearing was held early in October 1972. The Senate Committee on Communications, chaired by Senator Pastore, met to discuss the validity of the bill and the league's blackout policy. The justifications for the bill were really rather simple and obvious. Compared to the other major professional team sports, football contains relatively few games on its schedule. In 1972 the regular season consisted of fourteen games, which meant that each team played only seven regular-season home games a year. In addition, more than half the stadium seats were sold to season-ticket holders. To be precise, in 1972 season tickets made up 66% of the total stadium capacity in the American Football Conference and more than 74% in the National Football Conference.[7] Moreover, it was not uncommon for the strong teams to sell out their regular-season games weeks before kickoff.

Thus, the fact that the National Football League's blackout policy restricted games from being shown on local television meant that relatively few football fans were able to see their home team play half its schedule. To be sure, games were televised back to the visiting team's home territory, but all games were blacked out locally and usually sold out as well. In short, there were a great number of loyal football fans who were frustrated because they were unable to cheer their home teams either at the stadium or on their television sets. Senator Pastore remarked in his opening statement that he wanted passage so that "millions of fans will get a better shake."[8]

The antiblackout bill was also justified on the grounds that it would not go into effect unless the home game in question was sold out in advance. Indeed, this was a very important aspect of the law, because the blackout could be maintained by the league provided the game was not sold out by a certain time. This deadline was a matter of debate and would change over the months that followed, but the original bill called for a 48-hour limit. In other words, if tickets for the following Sunday's game remained unsold by Friday morning, then the blackout could remain intact, but if the game was sold out by Friday morning, the blackout would have to be lifted. This provision in the law made it extremely difficult to oppose.

Another rationale for the law was the treatment that Congress had afforded the National Football League in 1961 and 1966. Simply, congressmen would not allow the National Football League's commissioner, Pete Rozelle, to forget the favor they had done for him with the exemptions from the antitrust laws that allowed the National Football League to engage in package contracts with television networks, and subsequently to merge with the American Football

League. Senator Pastore claimed that because it had received previous exemptions, the National Football League had "the whole loaf" and did not "want to give the public a slice!"[9]

Nevertheless, the league bitterly fought the antiblackout bill on any grounds it could. Commissioner Pete Rozelle's opposition remained consistent, although at certain times it seemed more reasonable than at others. He invented all sorts of arguments to combat the bill, including a fear that lifting blackouts would cause strange situations at the ticket windows on Friday mornings as fans would be "scrambling for the end of the line" in hopes of getting to see the game for free on television."[10] Rozelle further believed that the bill would be self-defeating because it would lead to fewer sellouts; thus, the blackout would be intact in any case. Arguments such as these were simply "farfetched" to most of the congressmen and did not help the National Football League's case.

Yet Rozelle did raise some valid objections to the bill, which senators at least listened to. Without a doubt the most powerful argument Rozelle could rely on was the possibility of a sharp increase in "no-shows"—fans who bought tickets to the game, but decided to stay away from the stadium once they realized the game was sold out and could be seen in the comfort of their living rooms.[11] No-shows could affect professional football in a number of ways. Concessions and parking would be directly affected if a large number of ticket holders stayed home. Also, Rozelle correctly pointed out that fan emotion in the stands, a large part of the game, could diminish if the number of no-shows was high.[12]

These two points were part of a broader argument that an antiblackout law could transform professional football from a live spectator sport into a "studio" sport.[13] The fear was that the antiblackout law would discourage interest in seeing the games live, leading fans to view professional football on the small screen rather than at the stadium. Rozelle explained, "[W]hen people are accustomed to having something for free, they are not likely to be enthusiastic about paying for it on other occasions."[14] Theoretically, this would seriously damage gate revenues and change the entire character of professional football. Rozelle soon realized, however, that it was unrealistic to expect Congress to refrain from passing some sort of antiblackout legislation.

Witnesses representing the other major professional team sports also testified in October 1972. Don Ruck, vice-president of the

National Hockey League, had some reservations about the long-term effects of the bill, but stated that professional hockey would be willing to try it on an experimental basis.[15] Ruck had experience in his favor, inasmuch as the National Hockey League had tried lifting local blackouts on several occasions and had enjoyed limited success when it did so.[16] Of course, all four major professional team sports were free to utilize the blackout as a tool to insure the highest possible gate receipts, but in light of the relatively large number of games that were played by the other sports and the limited number of sellouts they enjoyed, the antiblackout legislation would not affect them nearly the same way it would professional football.

Commissioner Walter Kennedy testified on behalf of the National Basketball Association. Kennedy admitted that there was a lot of positive potential wrapped up in the bill if both gate receipts and television revenues could be maximized.[17] Nevertheless, he had reservations about the bill and stated that basketball was opposed to its passage until after a study could be conducted by the Federal Communications Commission.[18]

Commissioner Bowie Kuhn represented organized baseball. He opposed the bill, relying, as always, on the game's tradition of honorable self-regulation.[19] Kuhn argued that public interest alone should serve as the regulator of the market and not a federal statute.[20] All of the witnesses quickly realized, however, that they were fighting an uphill battle; the bill was simply too popular with the Congress's constituencies, as well as the White House. Yet, Congress failed to meet President Nixon's deadline; the 1972 season was played under the league's traditional blackout policy.

The issue was far from dead, however, and in the summer of 1973, Congress held another round of hearings. Massachusetts Representative Torbert H. MacDonald, chairman of the House Subcommittee on Communication and Power, set the tone of the hearings when he proclaimed that he was fed up with the "public-be-damned attitude" of the NFL.[21] As the proceedings opened on July 31, both sides dug in deep.

The subcommittee listened to a chorus of witnesses who opposed the antiblackout measure. NFL Commissioner Rozelle led the opposition. He reiterated all the concerns before the House that he had expressed in the Senate the previous year. Rozelle claimed that although he had "racked his brain" to find a compromise to please everyone, he could not rationalize a change in the NFL's broadcasting policies.[22] The NFL's commissioner also suggested that Congress could find better things to regulate than professional football, which ranked with the "rope and twine industry" in economic importance.[23]

The other professional sports held their ground as well. Bowie Kuhn again emphasized that the marketplace should be the sole determiner of broadcasting policies, and that if legislation was needed, it should not apply to organized baseball in any case.[24] Walter Kennedy cried that the legislation represented a "frontal attack" on "the life-blood of professional sports," that is, gate receipts, which he claimed were the "single most important source of a team's revenue."[25] While his claim was accurate with regard to professional basketball, it was no longer true for professional football. Finally, Don Ruck reaffirmed that the NHL would support temporary legislation, but only reservedly.[26] He added, "It took me a year to get to see [the Broadway musical] My Fair Lady, but I didn't . . . complain to get it on free t.v."[27]

Yet the officials within professional sports were alone in "left field."[28] On September 6, 1973, only eleven days before opening day for the NFL, the Senate passed the antiblackout legislation by a vote of 76 to 6. The House wasted no time acting on the measure, either, passing the bill by a vote of 336 to 37 on September 14.[29] One of the few dissenters, Republican Representative Jack Kemp of New York, a former AFL quarterback, claimed that "the Gulf of Tonkin Resolution was the last thing that passed the Congress this fast."[30] President Nixon enthusiastically added his signature and the bill became law on September 14, just three days before opening kickoff.[31]

The legislation was to be in effect for three years and was to be monitored during that time by the Federal Communications Commission. At the end of the 1975 season Congress would re-evaluate the law; any further action would be based on the findings of the FCC. The effect of the legislation was felt immediately; eight of the twelve home games on the opening day of the 1973 season were televised in local regions where they would have been blacked out a few days earlier.

Yet, as soon as the bill became law, critics began to surface, both inside and outside professional football. Some felt that Congress had overstepped its bounds with the passage of the antiblackout bill. Arthur Daley of the *New York Times* felt that Congress acted as if "free football is really an inalienable human right!"[32] "I believe that the American football fan is the most pampered, petted, spoiled species in the history of the world," wrote Robert Markus in the

Chicago Tribune.[33] As for the fans, one observed simply, "I've never figured out how you get a ticket. I'll enjoy seeing the games." "I mean this is a sport, isn't it?" chimed another fan. "They shouldn't care about the money."[34] James Reston commented that the anti-blackout law was the "most popular thing since the repeal of the Volstead Act," but feared that Congress was too freely giving away services that belonged to someone else.[35] Rozelle was relieved that the legislation was temporary, and remained determined to discredit it any way he could. For the time being, though, Rozelle, Congress, the press, and the fans could do no more than keep a close eye on the findings of the FCC with which the destiny of the antiblackout legislation lay.

The FCC monitored the antiblackout law closely during the 1973, 1974, and 1975 seasons. The commission filed an annual report each spring to disclose the effects of the legislation on the previous season. As expected, the commission discovered that the law did not have any significant impact on the other three professional team sports although technically it applied to them all. Also, as expected, the bill profoundly affected professional football. In 1973, for example, 109 of 182 regular season games were televised locally when a sellout lifted the blackout.[36]

The most important statistic that the commission monitored, however, was the no-show. Arguably, the behavior of this one statistic determined the life of the antiblackout legislation. The commission discovered that the law was not only safe for professional football, but that it was actually beneficial to the sport. In 1973, the no-shows for a locally televised game averaged 9.9%. For games that were blacked out locally in 1973, the average was about 9.2%. The gap closed even more in 1974, from 11.2% to 10.8%.[37] Then, in 1975, the FCC found that a decrease in no-shows had actually occurred because of the antiblackout law. During the 1975 season, there were on average 7.1% no-shows for games that were televised locally and 9.6% for games that were blacked out.[38]

The FCC's 1976 report declared that the law was not harmful in any way to professional football. On the contrary, greater television exposure had spawned greater fan interest, which had actually led to higher attendance at the stadium, not an increase in the number of no-shows. The report concluded that the antiblackout law had been "beneficial" not only to the fans, but to professional sports as well.[39] The NFL, however, was not convinced.

But for Congress, making the antiblackout law permanent was nearly a foregone conclusion. The Senate and the House held hearings on the issue in the fall of 1975, just before the 1973 law was to expire. The atmosphere in both chambers of Congress was the same. Virtually all members of Congress were convinced of the usefulness and validity of the legislation and felt that its passage was necessary.

Thus, when Rozelle again testified before the Senate, the event was really more of a formality than anything else. Nonetheless, the senators patiently listened to his pleas for mercy. The National Football League was still holding hopes of escaping any antiblackout legislation, at least of the permanent variety. The fact was, though, that professional football had no real ground on which to resist permanent antiblackout legislation. The FCC's reports represented the ultimate congressional reference for the antiblackout law, and that reference was, after all, a glowing one.

Although Rozelle grasped for a number of straws in his resistance to the antiblackout law, the most effective argument he could muster was a fear that the law would lead to an "erosion" of fan interest in attending football games.[40] Such "erosion" might lead professional football down the path of becoming little more than a "studio sport." This argument represented nothing new. All that Rozelle could really hope for was another temporary extension of the law. Relying on the FCC, the Senate quickly refuted the arguments of Rozelle. As the annual reports clearly showed, weather and team standings had more to do with no-shows than the antiblackout law.[41] Thus, in the FCC's view, there was no realistic chance of professional football's becoming a "studio sport."

Congress once again called in representatives from the other three major team sports to testify. Each witness expressed the same view and concerns: Although the antiblackout law had proven to be useful so far, its full impact had probably not yet been felt. In essence, these witnesses wanted an extension of the three-year law that was due to expire in December 1975. Finally, the representatives from the major television networks were all in favor of the legislation. In fact, the American Broadcasting Company even suggested trimming the time limit for a sellout back to 24 hours.[42] In short, Pete Rozelle was alone in his attack on the antiblackout legislation at the Senate hearings.

The House also held hearings a second time on the antiblackout bill. Again, Rozelle fought in vain against the bill, but his complaints did not receive the same indulgence in the House. The House Subcommittee on Communications, chaired by Torbert H. Mac-Donald of Massachusetts, was less than patient in listening to the complaints of Rozelle and the National Football League. In his opening statement, MacDonald disclosed his leanings when he declared that the antiblackout law was a "perfect" law because it was "self-correcting," it would only go into effect after a sellout had occurred.[43]

In fact, the subcommittee was rather belligerent toward Rozelle and the "business" of professional football. MacDonald declared that most of Rozelle's testimony was pure "baloney" and even went so far as to accuse him of questioning the integrity of the Federal Communications Commission.[44] Democratic Representative William M. Brodhead of Michigan probably reflected the sentiments of most members of Congress when he told Rozelle, "Frankly you're not getting much sympathy from me. I can't see where any business that pays it employees $40,000 and up for five months work can come in and cry poverty. . . . If you're losing money, its because the sport has been mismanaged."[45] As for the idea of another three-year extension, MacDonald asked Rozelle, "[D]o you really want to go through this charade every three years?"[46] In sum, Congress had seen enough and had made up its mind that a permanent antiblackout law needed to be passed before the end of the 1975 season.

Therefore, in the first week of December, the Senate passed by a voice vote the Sports Broadcasting Act of 1975. During the following week, on December 16, the House passed a similar bill by a 363-to-40 margin.[47] The laws differed in a couple of important respects, however. The House-passed bill was to be permanent and limited the range of blackouts, when they occurred, to 75 miles. The Senate version was a three-year extension that called for a limit of 120 miles.[48] As the old antiblackout bill was scheduled to expire on December 31, the replacement bills were rushed to a conference committee. But as the year trickled away, hopes for the passage of a permanent antiblackout law began to fade. The conferees failed to come up with a compromise bill, and the year ended without an extension of the law. Nonetheless, the NFL announced that it planned to abide by the terms of the expired law the following season. The league hoped to diffuse some of the tension between it and Congress and believed that its show of good faith might thwart permanent blackout legislation.[49]

Despite Rozelle's apparent concern for the public's interest, the conferees continued into the spring of 1976 to work for an extension of the antiblackout law. The conference committee claimed that it was waiting for the FCC's third annual report before making a final decision. The commission issued its report on June 10, and although it stated that the antiblackout law had not been harmful to the NFL, the conferees still could not reach an agreement.[50] The sticking point between the two houses remained the size of the blackout area and the question of whether the law should be permanent. On both issues, the Senate was clearly more sympathetic to the NFL than the House was. During the spring and summer of 1976, the NFL intensely lobbied the Senate.[51] Its efforts were ultimately successful; the conferees failed to produce a recommendation for legislation in the 94th Congress.

Much of the credit, or blame, for the failure of the antiblackout legislation lay with Washington Senator Warren Magnuson. Magnuson was the ranking member on the conference committee and the leading opponent of a permanent antiblackout bill. One report charged that Magnuson had worked to kill the legislation for the NFL and, in exchange, Seattle had received an expansion team.[52] The conferee chairman bitterly denied any such "corrupt bargain"; nevertheless, Seattle did get its team for the 1976 season. The league had announced as far back as June 1974 that Seattle and Tampa Bay would receive expansion teams; thus, it is unlikely that the NFL dealt Magnuson a quid pro quo. Yet, it is unbelievable that Magnuson's deliberate efforts to stall the antiblackout bill and Seattle's receipt of an NFL franchise were merely coincidental. If nothing else, the Washington senator was returning a favor to the league. Be that as it may, in 1976 the antiblackout law failed to become a permanent fixture in sports broadcasting.

Although the NFL continued to abide by the terms of the old blackout law through the 1976 and 1977 seasons, Congress refused to forget the legislation. The FCC monitored the effects of blackouts through 1976 and 1977; by the spring of 1978, the House was ready once again to hold hearings on the possible revival of the anti-blackout law.[53] On April 28, the Subcommittee on Communications, chaired by California Representative Lionel Van Deerlin, held one day of hearings.

The 1978 hearings were unique in that they took place in Dade County, Florida. The subcommittee was particularly interested in the antiblackout policy's impact on the Miami Dolphins. The FCC's first two reports had shown that, of all the teams in professional football, the antiblackout policy had done the most harm to the Miami Dolphins. Miami had suffered the greatest increase in no-shows and, thus, had lost the most money as a result of the legislation. The FCC claimed that the reasons for the increase in no-shows were a decline in the quality of the Dolphins' play and bad weather.[54] Indeed, while the Dolphins sold out only one game during the 1977 season, there were fewer no-shows for that televised game than for many games that were not televised. The FCC believed that this fact mitigated "the severity of the TV factor."[55] Nonetheless, the subcommittee was interested in hearing how the Miami Dolphins organization felt about the antiblackout policy.

Don Shula, head coach of the Dolphins, argued that the policy was partially to blame for the decline in the number of season tickets his team sold in 1977. In 1973, the Dolphins sold an NFL-record 74,961 season tickets, but in 1977 they sold fewer than 35,000. He claimed that no-shows turned into "no-buys"; as a result, the Dolphins lost their home-field edge. His team, Shula argued, found it more difficult to win at home because fewer fans showed up to cheer them on.[56]

Shula's testimony was reinforced by the statement of Dick Anderson, retired player and former president of the National Football League Players Association, who claimed, "from a player's standpoint, we need fans in the stadium."[57] Joseph Robbie, managing partner of the Dolphins, also testified in opposition to the policy. He blamed the antiblackout policy for the severe reduction in the Dolphins' season ticket sales and confessed that he did not understand the justification for the policy, because fans were able to watch all of their team's road games on television.[58]

All of the arguments and positions used in 1978 were nearly identical to those bandied about in 1972. Congress neither learned anything new in its 1978 hearing nor took a definite step toward enacting a piece of permanent antiblackout legislation. The 1978 hearings were the last ones Congress held to deal exclusively with the blackout issue. Ultimately, the NFL escaped without a permanent piece of legislation's being passed. But the league continued to follow the spirit of the old temporary antiblackout law that expired after the 1975 season. NFL fans continued to view their team's home games on television, provided the game was sold out before the 72-

hour deadline. In this case, the spirit of the law proved as effective as its letter; on balance, Congress's efforts proved productive.

The antiblackout controversy represented the last full-scale attempt by Congress to affect sports broadcasting. During the 1980s, however, Congress concerned itself with still another issue in professional sports broadcasting. In 1987–89 the Senate, with Howard Metzenbaum of Ohio leading the charge, held brief and legislatively fruitless hearings on the issue of cable television and professional sports.[59] As Metzenbaum summarized his concerns, "[T]he 1990s might become a decade in which fans must pay to watch any sport."[60] In sum, the question Congress has recently been asking about sports broadcasting is whether cable television will supplement or supplant regular network sports broadcasts.[61] While sports officials have promised Congress that an ample supply of games will be available on free television through this century, including playoffs, the Super Bowl, and the World Series, many fear that pay television will become the medium of choice in professional sports.[62]

In 1987, for the first time, the NFL negotiated a package agreement with the Entertainment and Sports Network (ESPN) to broadcast one game a week. Professional football has subsequently reached similar agreements with other cable networks.[63] The league has simultaneously featured cable games on a free channel to the home territories of the two teams involved, so as to ensure that home fans have access to the games on free television.[64] Organized baseball, also for the first time, negotiated a similar contract with ESPN for the 1990 season.

At the present time, cable television merely supplements the sports offered on network television. Nevertheless, the trend is toward pay television. In 1992 the NFL sent a trial balloon over Congress concerning plans to make games available to fans on a pay-per-view basis. These games would be in addition to regular network offerings, but the plan manifests the NFL's desire to get into pay television in a bigger way. Some members of Congress, such as Pennsylvania Senator Arlen Specter, reacted with strong opposition to the NFL's proposal. Specter maintained that it was wrong for the NFL to use any pay-per-view telecasts as long as it had its 1961 and 1966 antitrust exemptions. Indeed, the exemptions provide Congress with heavy leverage to force the league to keep public interest in the forefront of its broadcasting policy.[65]

And all of this does have an impact on public interest because many people either cannot afford cable television or do not have access to it because of geography. In light of Congress's track record on professional sports broadcasting, interested fans can be sure that members of Congress will assume active roles in the cable-broadcast controversy and possibly affect the outcome with legislation.

* * *

The most interesting and important observation to be made about Congress's treatment of professional sports broadcasting is that, with the exception of the controversy over the demise of the minor leagues, Congress repeatedly acted with a decisiveness absent in its dealings with professional sports and their legal positions under the antitrust laws. Organized baseball, of course, emerged unscathed from a more than a dozen hearings on its antitrust exemption held over a period of 40 years. Congress even allowed the sport to manage its own broadcasting affairs in the mid-1950s, when it seemed that such management was killing the minor leagues. The legislature's only moves in this area came in the form of a failed personal crusade by Senator Edwin C. Johnson. Congress has stepped very gingerly, when at all, regarding organized baseball. Professional football, on the other hand, received the opposite treatment from Congress. Laws were passed that effected significant change in the broadcasting of the sport. The explanation for this varying behavior can be found in the nature of the issue, the wording of the laws, and the character of the primary sport involved, professional football.

Sports broadcasting, by its nature, lends itself more to congressional action than does, for example, organized baseball's reserve clause. Telecasting and broadcasting of professional sports contests directly affect the public, the constituency of Congress. The blackout controversy, for instance, was highly publicized and the activities of Congress were watched carefully by sports fans across the country. The issue snowballed; its popularity may have rivaled the repeal of Prohibition. The controversy generated strong public opinion, and Congress naturally tends to act more decisively on issues perceived as directly affecting the public interest.[66]

Also, the wording of the laws passed on sports broadcasting explains congressional behavior. The 1961 law to allow package contracts between sports leagues and television networks was, after all, a permissive law that provided a limited exemption for professional sports. In other words, the law could not harm but only help sports leagues, including the American Football League, rival of the NFL. The antiblackout legislation was unlike the package-contract legislation in many ways. It was neither permissive in character nor popular with the leaders of professional sports. Nonetheless, the law was viewed by almost everyone as "self-correcting" or self-regulating. Too, the law was, at first, only temporary and was monitored by the Federal Communications Commission for its duration. These facts assured the public that Congress was not acting heavy-handedly or irresponsibly with professional sports. Thus, the built-in safety features of the antiblackout law further explain Congress's behavior in the realm of professional sports broadcasting.

Finally, the character and public image of professional football explain the actions of Congress. Professional football has never enjoyed baseball's aura of romanticism and tradition. Whereas Congress personified organized baseball as "the kid on the sandlot," professional football evoked images of the "forty-thousand-dollar quarterback." Moreover, while terms such as *clean* and *honest* characterized baseball in congressional hearings, other terms, such as *business* and *profit*, described football. Congress never handled professional football as an innocent sport that needed pampering. Even when Congress granted the game an exemption in 1961 for package deals, it did so as much to guarantee competition within the industry as anything else.

Rather, Congress has generally treated professional football as a multi-million-dollar business that needs monitoring. Its comparative lack of tradition in American life, its meteoric rise to wealth and popularity in the 1960s through a union with the television industry, its upper-class status symbol appeal in the early 1970s, and maybe even the strong, clever, but blatant business approach of Pete Rozelle —all explain Congress's view of professional football. And this view, as much as anything else, explains Congress's handling of the sport when it comes to broadcasting issues.

One can only speculate what further action Congress will take in regard to professional sports broadcasting. As mentioned, the advent of cable television and the NFL's pay-per-view proposal have already attracted the interest of members of Congress. In view of recent history, it is likely that whatever action Congress takes will be both quick and direct, because professional sports broadcasting plays too great a role in American life for Congress to remain passive in relation to its development.

PART III

Congress, League Mergers, and Franchise Relocations

Chapter 8

The End-Runs, 1966–72

On June 8, 1966, Pete Rozelle, commissioner of the National Football League, and Lamar Hunt, commissioner of the American Football League, announced that their leagues had reached a merger agreement, which was to go into effect before the start of the 1970 season.[1] The purpose of the merger was to end the bidding war for player talent that had developed between the NFL and AFL. Franchises in both leagues had been doling out huge signing bonuses (some near $600,000) and record salaries to untried rookies.[2]

Although there were numerous points to the agreement, the most important provisions were for a combined draft, a two-team expansion by 1968, and an interleague world championship game that was scheduled for the end of the 1966 season. The leagues decided to retain Rozelle as commissioner for both leagues and to keep all existing franchises at their current locations.[3]

The announcement created a great deal of excitement and publicity. It appeared that the AFL, after only seven years of existence, had finally won the respect of the 46-year-old NFL. Over the last few seasons, the quality of play in the AFL compared to the NFL had been a topic of debate among football fans, and the prospect of an interleague championship game sparked a great deal of interest. But the league commissioners believed that the merger had little chance of standing up under the antitrust laws without some type of congressional protection or immunity. Rozelle and Hunt claimed that they did not expect Congress to grant their leagues a carte blanche immunity but only a limited exemption for their merger. Without such an exemption, the merger would be vulnerable to the Sherman Act, because it would eliminate all competition for football talent and create an unquestionable monopoly.[4] Indeed, immediately following their announcement, a group of businessmen in Chicago filed an antitrust suit against the two leagues. The businessmen were providing the financial support for a proposed expansion team for the AFL.[5]

113

Rozelle, therefore, was quick to petition Congress for an antitrust exemption for his merger plans. He received a warm reception in the Senate; a bill was introduced by Senators Russell Long of Louisiana and Everett Dirksen of Illinois to grant the NFL and AFL their exemption. The bill sought to legalize a common draft and, as a condition for allowing the merger, provided the same protection from professional football broadcasts to high schools that had been given to colleges in 1961.[6] The legislation was hurriedly approved by the full Judiciary Committee and sent to the floor of the Senate for a vote.[7] On September 26, 1966, the Senate passed the measure by a voice vote.[8]

Rozelle was not greeted so warmly in the House, where the merger bill cruised into a brick wall that was built primarily by Emanuel Celler, chairman of the Judiciary Committee. Celler had gained a reputation as an opponent of professional sports in the 1950s after his bouts with organized baseball. He had played an important role in 1961 when Congress granted an antitrust exemption to professional sports for package broadcasting deals. Nevertheless, the purpose of the 1961 exemption was to maintain competition between the NFL and AFL, and Celler made it clear in the fall of 1966 that he was not going to allow a merger between the leagues without a fight.[9]

Celler's constituents were divided over the issue. One wrote, "I seem to sense that you are not letting yourself get pushed around by Pete Rozelle and his 260 pound tackles. Power to you."[10] But another told Celler, "You enjoyed my vote, now let me enjoy my football."[11] Nevertheless, the chairman of the Judiciary Committee scheduled hearings on the bill and generally did his best to stall the legislation every way that he could.

Then on October 7, Donald F. Turner, assistant U.S. attorney general, announced that if no protective legislation were granted to the merger plan, numerous lawsuits would undoubtedly result.[12] Rozelle also reiterated his fears of "endless litigation" and promised that the NFL and AFL would not effect their merger plan without a legislative exemption.[13] That was a calculated move by Rozelle to urge congressional action by playing on the fears of a public now enthralled with the idea of an interleague championship game for the 1966 season. The statement was also a last-ditch effort to save the merger legislation, which seemed less likely each day to pass the House.

Celler's delay tactics proved successful, despite the fact that a majority within his committee supported the legislation. He was upset that the Senate did not hold hearings on the legislation, and declared that he planned "to plumb the depths" of the merger plan before granting it an antitrust exemption.[14] Time was on Celler's side, and the merger probably would not have materialized had not been for some slick parliamentary maneuvering in the Senate. The bill's co-sponsors in the Senate, Dirksen and Long, devised a plan to attach the football merger bill as a rider to another piece of legislation that was a shoo-in for passage, the Investment Tax Credit bill. The move was a blatant attempt to make an "end run" around Celler's committee.[15]

The Investment Tax Credit bill was an anti-inflationary measure that President Lyndon Johnson had been asking Congress to pass for some time. As expected, the tax bill, with the attached rider exempting the football merger, passed both houses, but in different versions; it was then sent to a conference committee. Senator Long headed the Senate conferees, each of whom represented a district that either already had a professional football team or wanted to obtain one in the future.[16] Thus, the merger rider survived the conference committee, and the bill was sent to the floor of the House for a vote.

There was little that Celler could do. Because the bill had already passed both houses and had endured a conference committee, it could not be returned to the House Judiciary Committee for hearings or approval.[17] The only way that the merger could be blocked would be for the entire tax bill to be voted down in the House. Celler attempted to have the measure amended on the floor, but his efforts were easily shot down by the merger's proponents, which included Louisiana Representative Hale Boggs. "The end run was not made around me," Celler claimed, "the end run was made around the public . . . and the players."[18] He further vowed (mixing his sports metaphors), "I may lose this game, but I won't lose the series."[19] Boggs blamed Celler's failure to achieve a thorough round of hearings on his own desire to see the bill defeated. Moreover, Boggs did not feel that professional football should be penalized for Celler's tactics of procrastination.[20]

Following this debate on October 20, the bill passed easily, 161 to 76. Interestingly, Celler's animosity toward the football merger was not enough to keep him from voting for the Investment Tax Credit bill. The Senate approved the measure the following day.[21] And on November 8, President Johnson signed the bill into law, clearing the way for the NFL-AFL merger and the first interleague championship game.[22]

"All I want is one of LBJ's pens," said Pete Rozelle, referring to President Johnson's custom of distributing among a bill's supporters the personalized pens he used to sign a measure into law.[23] Rozelle and the NFL were so pleased with the efforts of Senator Long and Representative Boggs that they announced on November 1 that New Orleans would be the proud recipient of a football franchise in 1967.[24] That was welcome news to Boggs, who was in the midst of a tough reelection campaign.[25] As for the 78-year-old Celler, he never did resume his fight against the merger and, indeed, lost the "series" as well as the "game."

While the NFL and AFL were fighting for their merger in 1966, the American Basketball Association (ABA) had come into being to compete with the established National Basketball Association. The fact that the new league was formed in 1966 was not merely coincidental; the ABA was a direct response to the AFL's successful attempt to effect a merger with the NFL.[26] The ABA was actually more successful in the initial stages leading to a merger than the AFL. And by 1970, the ABA had forced the NBA to the table to iron out a merger plan. The ABA's strategy was time-worn: a draft and salary war that had driven the median salary in professional basketball up from $23,000 to $43,000.[27] Thus, early in 1971, the leagues announced plans to merge before the 1973 season.[28]

However, on April 16, 1970, Oscar Robertson, president of the NBA Players Association, filed suit against the NBA's merger plan on the grounds that a merger would strip the players of their freedom to sell their talent to the highest bidder.[29] Robertson's case would not be settled until 1975, when it effectively abolished the game's perpetual reserve clause.[30] But in the spring of 1971, basketball's officialdom was primarily concerned about the impact the case could have on their merger plans. In fact, the suit forced the NBA and ABA to seek out congressional relief in the form of an antitrust exemption similar to that granted to professional football five years earlier. Congress responded in 1971-72 with a pair of legislative hearings, one in each house.

Yet, the merger exemption never developed the kind of momentum that the football merger did, either in Congress or with the public; and it failed to come close to a vote in either house. The basketball merger had a number of things working against it. First,

Philip Hart, the chairman of the Senate Subcommittee on Anti-Trust and Monopoly, decided against presiding over the basketball merger hearings because he feared that some might accuse him of a conflict of interest because of his personal connections to professional sports.[31] Back in 1961, when asked about his role in the package-broadcasting legislation, Hart had responded, "[T]he fact that I had been a sitting duck for a charge of 'conflict of interest' didn't bother my conscience a bit."[32] Ten years later, however, he was more sensitive about his personal ties to professional sports. Therefore, he left Sam Ervin of North Carolina in charge of the basketball hearings. Whereas Hart had a reputation for being kind to professional sports, Ervin made it clear from the start that he was concerned about the "evils of big sports monopolies."[33]

Aside from a belligerent chairman, the basketball merger had to contend with poor timing. In September 1971, organized baseball announced that the Washington Senators were moving to Texas. The Senators' move upset many members of Congress and generally created an atmosphere on Capitol Hill that was not conducive to favors for professional sports leagues of any type.[34]

Thus, it surprised no one when Senator Ervin opened the 1971 hearings with strong words against the proposed merger. He declared that the concept of a merger was a violation of the antitrust laws because a merger would eliminate all competition for players, relegating them to mere "chattel."[35] Ervin also argued that the common draft was an "evil, binding thing" that would only serve the "pocketbooks of owners." Finally, he believed that the football merger had been "railroaded" through Congress. Ervin was determined that the same treatment would not be afforded to the planned basketball merger.[36]

Other legislators, however, could see the positive potential of a merger, as it would end the bidding war and stop the allegedly imminent bankruptcy of the leagues. Ultimately, the success of the merger bill depended on this one issue. In short, the owners of both leagues were crying to Congress for merciful intervention to end the ruinous bidding war. Senator Ervin did not buy their argument, however, nor did the majority of players who testified at the hearings held in the House and Senate.

Oscar Robertson spoke on behalf of the NBA Players Association. He firmly opposed the bill because he believed a merger would end the bargaining freedom that professional basketball players enjoyed. Robertson predicted that player salaries would spiral down to unacceptable levels if a merger were effected.[37] Bill Bradley, a player for the New York Knicks and a co-plaintiff in Robertson's suit with the NBA, agreed. He claimed that the players preferred to continue without a merger. Bradley also argued that a merger would violate the "constitutional fundamentals of the Nation."[38]

Lawrence Fleisher, counsel for the players association, testified that the consensus among the players was that a merger would do them harm. He also used race as a weapon, warning congressmen that their treatment of the issue was being carefully watched by black Americans, in particular, because 65% of NBA rosters consisted of blacks.[39] Not since the 1939 anti-fight-film hearings had race been such an important issue in a congressional hearing on professional sports. Senator Edward Kennedy was reportedly upset when he learned that he had been listed as a co-sponsor of the merger legislation, because he did not want to appear antiblack.[40]

The most damaging testimony against the bill came not from a basketball player, but from a football player named John Mackey. Mackey played for the Baltimore Colts and served as the president of the NFL Players Association. He was convinced that the NFL-AFL merger had already seriously harmed football players. Mackey argued that the elimination of the AFL had diminished the bargaining power of players and led to a sharp decline in salaries.[41] Ed Garvey, executive director for the NFL Players Association, also opposed the merger bill because it would create a situation where the "individual player is an extremely small economic unit confronting a vast, unregulated monopoly."[42] The testimonies of Mackey and Garvey served to reinforce Senator Ervin's misgivings about the bill.

Still, Congress could not allow a number of professional basketball franchises to go bankrupt because of players' demands for higher salaries. This is exactly what the owners, and some players, claimed would happen if a merger were not effected. Rick Barry, a star for the ABA's New York Nets, testified that maintenance of the status quo would result in the demise of the sport. He told the subcommittee that the "astronomical salaries that are being handed out to untried ballplayers" created hard feelings among veteran players and crippled teams financially. Any player opposition to the merger, he concluded, was driven by self-interest rather than an interest for the game.[43] However, it is interesting to note that several months after his testimony, Barry sent the Senate a letter in which, while he reiterated his support for a merger, he also encouraged Congress to force the leagues to do away with their established option and reserve systems.[44]

The game's ownership was represented at the hearings by Thomas H. Kuchel, a former U.S. senator from California and a current Washington, D.C., attorney. Kuchel predicted that Congress would decide whether professional basketball would "flourish or fail." According to the former senator, the "ever-escalating bidding war" had thrown the sport into "deep economic trouble."[45] In brief hearings held before the House, Kuchel stated that the rivalry between the ABA and NBA had produced "amazing and unbelievable" contracts for "untried rookies." He also claimed that players' salaries accounted for more than 65% of the total operating cost of a professional basketball team, while in football they represented only 25–35% of the total operating cost.[46]

The commissioners of the two leagues also testified in support of the merger. Walter Kennedy, commissioner of the NBA, stated that the two leagues were "destroying each other" through their bidding war.[47] And Jack Dolph, commissioner of the ABA, feared for the future of the league, which he claimed was in "peril." The "situation is not merely serious—it is critical. . . . To delay action is to invite destruction," Dolph warned.[48] A report by *U.S. News* confirmed many of the concerns held by the bill's advocates. The magazine recorded that the average salary among NBA players was $50,000, the highest among all the professional sports. Moreover, professional basketball was the biggest financial loser among the professional team sports; only 3 of 28 teams, the magazine estimated, made money during the 1970 season.[49]

Congress was not persuaded by the owners' pleas for mercy. Rather, legislators believed that the game's financial woes could be solved not by decreasing player salaries but by reforming the gate-receipt sharing system used by the leagues. Under professional basketball's existing operations, the visiting team did not receive any proceeds from ticket sales. Thus, an ABA team that played in an arena with a seating capacity of 7,000 was at a huge disadvantage in relation to a team such as the NBA's New York Knicks, who played in Madison Square Garden with a capacity of almost 20,000.[50] In professional football, on the other hand, the visiting team received 40% of the proceeds from ticket sales; in baseball the figure was 20%.[51] Congress became convinced that this was creating the financial demise of particular basketball teams, not the player-bidding war.

Thus, when the Senate Subcommittee on Anti-Trust and Monopoly finally reported a merger bill to the full Judiciary Committee, the bill carried an amendment that would force professional basketball to adopt a new gate-sharing system, allowing at least 30% of the proceeds to go to the visiting team.[52] A number of other criteria had to be met as well. One of the criteria would have eliminated any type of reserve system in professional basketball as well as any type of compensation rule or "Rozelle Rule."[53] However, the bill did provide for a unified draft. Also, there could be no reduction in the number of teams in operation; rather, Congress encouraged the leagues to expand.[54]

Needless to say, Congress's conditions for a merger were less than acceptable to either the NBA or the ABA.[55] Even if the merger bill were passed, the NBA would not merge with the ABA under such restraints. The NBA did not have to worry, however, because the merger bill never came close to passing in either house of Congress. By the 1976 season, the ABA had dissolved and four of its strongest franchises had joined the NBA to form a 22-team league.[56] Thus, the final result was still the elimination of the bidding war and a merger of sorts between the NBA and ABA; indeed, basketball executed its own "end run" around congressional resistance.

*   *   *

In the span of six years, Congress had dealt with two league merger attempts within professional sports and treated them in opposite manners. Professional football's merger proposal nearly sailed through both houses of Congress. Professional basketball, on the other hand, watched its merger proposal stall almost before it got started. There are several reasons for Congress's inconsistent behavior.

First, excepting Emanuel Celler, virtually no one, either inside or outside professional football, opposed the merger of the AFL and the NFL. In fact, the public seemed generally to support the legislation since it would allow the long-awaited interleague championship game. Also, professional football players were insufficiently organized to lobby against the bill in Congress. Besides, the consensus, even among player representatives, was that the merger would eliminate extraordinarily high signing bonuses and increase the median player salary. Jack Kemp, AFL Players Association president, declared, "I think the merger is in the best interest of the players, the fans, and the owners."[57]

There was another good reason to allow the merger, particularly for a congressman from southern Louisiana. New Orleans had been courting the NFL for some time in an effort to obtain a professional football franchise. That congressional representatives from Louisiana guided the football merger bill through to passage is not coincidental with New Orleans's obtaining a franchise for the 1967 season. In sum, the NFL used potential franchise expansions as carrots to motivate Congress to approve its proposed merger with the AFL, a luxury that professional basketball did not have in the early 1970s.

As for the image of the sport, its "business" character was not as fully developed in 1966 as it would be by the early 1970s and the blackout controversy; thus, Congress was willing to grant football an antitrust exemption. Moreover, football was arguably the most popular of all the professional team sports in the mid-1960s. Although during the later blackout controversy, the game's popularity was a disadvantage, in this case the sport's popularity worked to its advantage.

Professional basketball, on the other hand, was no higher than three on the professional sports totem pole—behind football and baseball—when it came to Congress for antitrust protection for its proposed merger.[58] Fewer people seemed interested in the basketball merger than had been interested in the football merger. The idea of an interleague basketball championship game or any type of interleague play simply did not generate the excitement for basketball that it had generated for football. In sum, professional basketball failed to bring the same type of strong public pressure to bear on Congress in 1971 that professional football had exerted in 1966.

Aside from the game's public status, there are several other reasons for the failure of basketball's proposed merger. As alluded to earlier, the timing of the announcement and hearings was terrible, just preceding the migration to Texas of baseball's Senators. Too, Senator Hart's unwillingness to chair the hearings doomed the merger bill from the start. Another very important reason for the failure of the basketball merger was that in 1971 professional basketball players were well organized and could offer strong resistance to the bill. Football players aided their basketball counterparts by effectively convincing Congress that its actions in 1966 had been detrimental to them. Many legislators came to view the football merger exemption as a mistake not to be repeated. Thus, the explanation for Congress's inconsistent treatment of the proposed football and basketball mergers lies in a number of places, including parliamentary maneuvering, player unification or the lack thereof, timing and circumstances, as well as the public perception and status of the professional sports in question.

Chapter 9

I Saw Brooklyn Die, 1981–85

Although the professional sports franchise relocation issue did not captivate Congress until the early 1980s, the movements of such businesses have caught the attention of sports fans throughout the post-World War II era. Indeed, the franchise relocations of the 1980s were nothing new to the sports world; during the period from 1950 to 1982, organized baseball experienced 11 team relocations, while football witnessed 13 such moves. During the same period, hockey saw 14 of its teams relocate and basketball endured 40 franchise relocations.[1] Until 1982, the various professional sports leagues controlled franchise movements through an approval vote by team owners. One reason for the 1964 congressional hearing on organized baseball's exemption from the antitrust laws was to discuss the controversy surrounding the American League's block of Charles Finley's plans to move his Kansas City Athletics to California. Congress discussed other franchise relocation controversies between 1950 and 1982, but only as peripheral issues.

In 1982, however, Congress began a string of congressional hearings devoted to the subject of franchise relocations. The hearings were prompted by an episode in professional football that concerned Al Davis, president of the NFL's Oakland Raiders. In 1981 Davis announced that he planned to move his team to the Los Angeles area because civic authorities in Oakland were not meeting his expectations regarding playing facilities.[2] When Davis's plans came before NFL owners for a vote, the league turned them down. The Los Angeles Memorial Coliseum, which would have housed Raiders games, proceeded to sue the league for unreasonable restraint of trade and violation of the antitrust laws.[3] Pete Rozelle, commissioner of the NFL, feared the possible outcome of the case and quickly began petitioning Congress for some legislative exemption for his league's relocation policy that would force the Raiders to remain in Oakland. Congress responded in 1982 with several bills and legislative hearings.

Senators Dennis DeConcini of Arizona and Arlen Specter of Pennsylvania introduced bills that addressed the franchise relocation issue. The Specter bill aimed to set up criteria for team movements within professional football, such as proof that the team had lost money for three consecutive years and that the playing facilities were inadequate. The DeConcini bill, on the other hand, would have given an antitrust exemption to all sports leagues, allowing them to manage the locations of their franchises without fear of litigation. The DeConcini bill had a counterpart in the House, sponsored by more than 130 representatives.[4] The Specter bill placed the onus on the team and league to prove economic hardship before a relocation would be allowed, while DeConcini's simply gave another antitrust exemption to professional sports officialdom to handle the matter the way they saw fit.

In fall 1982, the Senate Subcommittee on Anti-Trust and Monopoly, chaired by Strom Thurmond of South Carolina, listened to testimony from NFL representatives on the franchise relocation issue. Commissioner Rozelle testified that the NFL endorsed the DeConcini approach. He reiterated much of what he had said a few weeks earlier while testifying before a House subcommittee on the issue of baseball's exemption from the antitrust laws.[5] Rozelle stated that the NFL did not like the idea of Congress's arbitrarily creating criteria for franchise relocations. He argued that financial requirements could easily be met by team owners through a little tampering with the team's books. Each situation was unique and, said Rozelle, the most well-equipped body to decide on a proposed move was the sports league itself. He added that the Specter approach would create too much antitrust litigation and uncertainty, something any congressional act should seek to reduce.

Rozelle also assured Congress that the league was not seeking a blanket exemption for all its activities, but simply one that would solidify its authority over individual owners.[6] After all, until Davis's bold moves, the league's authority on the matter had been taken for granted, and there was no doubt where the league stood on Davis's proposed move because the owners had voted unanimously to block the proposal. In short, the NFL was simply lobbying Congress for a particular antitrust exemption to cover a policy in place since the league's inception.[7] It was widely known that Phoenix, Arizona, had desired an NFL franchise for several years; some charged that the senator from Arizona was in the back pocket of the NFL. But other legislators, including Senator Specter, voiced doubts about the accuracy of the charges, which faded quickly after no facts surfaced to support them.[8]

Al Davis also testified in fall 1982 before the Senate subcommittee. Davis claimed that he was willing to live with whatever decision Congress made, but he added that he opposed the DeConcini bill because it left franchise relocations up to the "whim or caprice" of team owners.[9] He believed that the Specter bill was a move in the right direction, as it tried to protect the public interest as well as the sport.[10]

As for his problems with the city of Oakland and the league, Davis told the subcommittee that he had lost close to $5 million in revenues because the Oakland authorities would not improve Alameda County Coliseum, which had been the home field of the Raiders since 1966. The Raiders owner argued that his organization was at a disadvantage; despite his personal affection for the people in Oakland, relocating his team afforded the best opportunities for winning. He also disagreed with the NFL's traditional argument that the league needed to be treated as one entity, reminding the subcommittee that the only revenues shared equally were those gleaned from package-television deals; teams did not share any other revenues and should be treated as individual units.[11]

Other witnesses also testified in support of the Specter bill. Ed Garvey and Gene Upshaw, representing the NFL Players Association, bitterly opposed the DeConcini bill. Garvey refused even to use the term "league" and continually labeled the NFL a "monopoly." He claimed that trusting the league to manage its own affairs with regard to team relocations was absolute "folly."[12] Upshaw said simply, "The NFL effort offends me as a citizen of this country. . . . I cannot believe that you will now give a blank check to these people again."[13] The extraordinarily belligerent attitudes of Garvey and Upshaw can be understood in light of the fact that as the congressional hearing was taking place, the NFL was involved in a bitter labor dispute that had culminated in a player walkout on September 20.[14]

Howard Cosell also testified on the relocation issue in the House. He remained as obstinate toward league officials in 1982 as he had been in 1972, and he "unreservedly" endorsed congressional efforts to regulate the movement of team franchises.[15] A sport, said Cosell, "invades the psyche of the people of a city. I saw Brooklyn die when the Dodgers left it."[16]

Nevertheless, despite all of the publicity surrounding the Raiders' proposed move, the hearings held in both houses, and the wide support within Congress for the DeConcini bill, no piece of franchise relocation legislation passed during 1982.

In 1984 the courts ruled in favor of Davis and the Los Angeles Coliseum. The NFL could not reverse the Raiders' move to southern California without some type of antitrust exemption from Congress.[17] The Raiders' success emboldened other team owners to attempt moves. In 1984 the Baltimore Colts became the Indianapolis Colts in what was described as a move made "in the middle of the night."[18] And in January 1985 Pete Rozelle received letters from the New Orleans Saints and the St. Louis Cardinals, informing him that they reserved the right to relocate whenever they wished, and were seriously considering doing so.[19] Besides the franchise instability within the NFL, the NBA also experienced an unapproved relocation in April 1984 when the Clippers moved from San Diego to Los Angeles.

The result of all this instability within professional sports was another series of hearings on the franchise relocation issue. The 1984 and 1985 hearings can be treated as a group because they were all called to deal with the same problems within professional sports, and they all had to do with bills that fell into one of two categories. The first type of bill, sponsored again by Senator DeConcini, among others, delegated sole responsibility to the league for the regulation of franchise movements. The second type of legislation placed responsibility on both the league and a federally appointed arbitration board.[20] In 1984 and 1985 a number of bills were introduced in Congress; each had its own characteristics (for example, some sought retroactively to force the Colts and Raiders back to their original cities), but all fell into one of the above two categories. The purpose of the bills, as Senator Thomas Eagleton of Missouri put it, was to stop teams from "cavalierly" moving and "leaving in their wake a financially or otherwise distraught community."[21]

League officials, from the various sports, testified in favor of the first type of relocation bill. Pete Rozelle argued that a federal arbitration board was "unnecessary and inappropriate" because the NFL had always been an outspoken critic of team relocations.[22] He blamed the current instability within professional sports on the Raiders' suit and Congress's failure to grant the leagues the power to enforce their relocation policies. Jay Moyer, counsel to the NFL, also pointed to the league's exemplary behavior regarding franchise movements. The league, said Moyer, could stabilize the sport if Congress would return the "tools" taken from it as a result of the Raiders' litigation. Rozelle also reminded Congress that "when we have stability, we will expand."[23] Thus, the league was again attempting to use expansion as a carrot to get Congress to do what it wanted.

Other sports officials agreed with Rozelle. James Fitzpatrick, testifying on behalf of baseball Commissioner Bowie Kuhn, opposed the idea of a federal arbitration board and suggested that Congress would be wise to leave the jurisdiction of team relocations solely within the leagues.[24] Philip Hochberg, counsel for the NBA, testified that professional basketball would only support legislation to leave responsibility for managing team movements within the league. As the NBA summarized its position, the decision "properly rests within the sound discretion of the league, and should not be subject to rigid federal regulation."[25]

Finally, John Ziegler, president of the National Hockey League, argued that a federal arbitration board would be too costly and time-consuming. Ziegler stated, "[C]larity is needed in this area, not more regulation."[26] In short, professional sports leagues tended to support the DeConcini approach to the problem and to oppose any approach that would strip or hinder their authority to decide the fate of proposed franchise relocations.

Municipal officials and the players themselves, on the other hand, lacked faith in the league and generally supported the idea of a federal arbitration board to determine whether or not a franchise movement was justified. Donald Schaefer, mayor of Baltimore, supported a bill introduced by Representative Barbara Mikulski of Maryland that would have forced the Colts to return to Baltimore and created a three-person federal arbitration board to decide relocation disputes in the future.[27] Mayor Schaefer maintained that the "roots" of the Colts were "sunk deeply into the community"and that their move had been a "heart wrenching, disturbing experience."[28] He also claimed that the loss of the Colts would cost the city's economy some $25–30 million annually.[29]

As for the players, Gene Upshaw of the NFL Players Association testified that his organization supported the formation of a federal arbitration board because it would not grant the league another antitrust exemption. Upshaw further suggested that the arbitration panel should have greater powers than those previously discussed, such as the power to subpoena witnesses and take testimony under oath.[30] Donald Fehr, executive director of the Major League Baseball Players Association, also opposed any legislation that would grant the leagues a new antitrust exemption. He argued that Congress should remove his sport's historic antitrust exemption; that, Fehr believed, would create healthy competition and rapid league expansion.[31] Thus, the proponents of a federal arbitration board also found a way to use league expansion as an incentive for Congress to pass their type of bill. Again, however, despite the testimonies of league officials, player representatives, and city leaders, Congress failed to act on a piece of franchise relocation legislation in either 1984 or 1985.

* * *

One result of Congress's legislative inaction with regard to the franchise relocation issue was that in 1988 the NFL's Cardinals flew from St. Louis to a sunnier field in Phoenix. While the Cardinals' flight has been the only team movement in professional football since the 1985 hearings concluded, rumors of franchise shifts in other sports continue to get Congress's attention. One reason for Senator Howard Metzenbaum's 1992 hearings on organized baseball's antitrust exemption was the Giants' proposed move from San Francisco to the Tampa Bay–St. Petersburg area. Certainly, the issue directly affects the public. As Senator John C. Danforth of Missouri put it, normally Congress would not concern itself with the movement of a business, but sports franchises are different because when they move, they carry the "support, identity, and spirit" of a community with them.[32]

In the coming years, the primary issue that Congress will have to decide is who will control the movement of franchises. For now, except in organized baseball, individual team owners have the final say; but the courts granted them their power just as they granted baseball its antitrust exemption, and the issue begs for legislative clarity. Like the cable television controversy, however, the franchise relocation issue is relatively new to Congress, and it is too early to draw conclusions on the matter. Some have suggested that Congress is most likely going to do nothing at all, because the issue is so volatile that any action would bring tremendous outcry from some part of the public.[33] Such a prediction is plausible, because Congress has failed to move authoritatively regarding professional sports when clear public support was lacking. Yet, the issue directly affects large segments of the American public, and Congress has tended to move on issues that stir public interest. Next to the issue of cable broadcasting and professional sports, the franchise relocation issue will present Congress with a huge and unavoidable challenge in the future.

Conclusion

Organized baseball represents an anomaly in more than one respect. The game obviously sits in a unique position under the antitrust laws because of its 1922 Supreme Court–granted exemption. But the sport represents an anomaly in another sense as well. That is, Congress has viewed and handled baseball differently from the other major professional sports. Members of Congress and baseball representatives repeatedly have pointed to the game's long tradition of honest and capable self-regulation, and have associated all that was good in America with the game. In 1953, Senator Edwin C. Johnson declared, "Baseball is democracy in action. . . . On the diamond, no questions are asked about which side of the railroad tracks a player comes from, or who his parents might have been. . . . Here men of all colors, races, national origins, and religions meet on a common ground."[1]

In short, many members of Congress have felt that organized baseball deserved a status above the law. The few legislators who believed otherwise, such as Representative Emanuel Celler and Senator Estes Kefauver, were consistently frustrated by the game's appeal as the national pastime and its deep-rooted place in American life. Baseball's image has changed since the idyllic days of the 1950s, along with the rest of professional sports; nevertheless, organized baseball continues to enjoy complete exemption from the nation's antitrust laws.

Professional boxing has had much less success in the halls of Congress than has organized baseball. The fight game came under heavy scrutiny and attack from people within and without Congress. The national legislature never seriously considered antitrust exemption for boxing; indeed, Congress came very close on several occasions to creating a federal board to regulate the sport. Still, Congress has refrained from doing so primarily because of the sport's image. While boxing has had its days in the sun, specifically in the period from 1920 to the early 1940s, the sport most often found itself only a step ahead of the law and abolitionist reformers. Crime figures and some of the athletes have periodically, but regularly, surfaced to

131

tarnish the sport's public image. Boxing's poor public image has motivated Congress to investigate the sport; yet, it was also the fight game's image as the "red light district" of professional sports that kept Congress from creating a federal boxing commission.

Professional football has enjoyed mixed success on Capitol Hill. The sport received limited exemptions in 1961 and 1966 that allowed for package television contracts and a league merger. Both exemptions have been vital to the growth of the sport. But professional football has never come close to receiving the sweeping antitrust exemption that organized baseball enjoys. And, of course, in the early 1970s professional football engaged Congress in a bitter struggle over its blackout policies. Technically, the game won; practically, professional football lost, as fear of congressional action forced the NFL to change its broadcasting policies voluntarily. Again, the explanation for Congress's behavior lies in the public image of the sport. Professional football cannot rely on a long tradition like baseball's. Moreover, the sport became a multi-million-dollar business seemingly overnight in the mid-1960s. To be sure, the game has enjoyed tremendous popularity, even to the point that many in the early 1970s argued that it had replaced baseball as the national pastime. But popularity did not always work in the interests of the sport. Rather, it aided congressional pressure, which led to a change in the game's blackout policies. Overall, Congress has tended to view professional football as a business requiring a watchful eye and occasional regulation.

Professional basketball has experienced even less success in Congress than professional football. Basketball fought only one major battle to gain an antitrust exemption for its proposed league merger. One of the explanations for the failure of the merger plan in Congress was basketball's lack of tradition in American life. The sport simply could not generate the kind of public support or wield the sword of tradition that benefited organized baseball. The timing of the merger plan was terrible; professional basketball was too young and inexperienced to push the plan through Congress.

As for professional hockey, it has received relatively little attention from Congress. In fact, Congress never has held a hearing that dealt directly with professional hockey. While the game surfaced regularly on the periphery of hearings on other sports, most of Congress's contact with hockey has been brief and insignificant. The reason is that hockey is historically a Canadian game and has been played in the United States mostly by Canadians or Europeans. Its role in American life has been relatively small, as has been its role in the relationship between Congress and professional sports.

Thus, the image of the particular professional sport in question was a decisive factor in determining congressional behavior. Each sport has its own public image and each sport has been handled differently by Congress. In every case, other factors, such as circumstances and politics, helped to determine congressional behavior, but the transcendent factor has been the image of the professional sport.

Congress and professional sports have developed a checkered relationship over the past 40 years. At times Congress has been quite friendly to the institution of professional sports, at other times downright unfriendly. Although most sports fans are unaware of this long and complex relationship, it represents a crucial series of episodes in sports history. In light of recent unresolved issues, such as cable television's effect on sports broadcasting and franchise relocations, maybe the best conclusion is that the relationship between Congress and professional sports will persist well into the next century. It simply cannot be otherwise because of the huge role that professional sports play in American life.

Notes

Introduction

1. David B. Truman, *The Governmental Process* (New York: Alfred A. Knopf, 1963), 369–91; William L. Morrow, *Congressional Committees* (New York: Charles Scribner's Sons, 1969), 372–77; Ralph K. Huitt, "The Congressional Committee, A Case Study," *American Political Science Review* 48 (June 1954), 340–65; see also, Woodrow Wilson, *Congressional Government: A Study in American Politics* (reprint, New York: World, 1956); George Goodwin, Jr., *The Little Legislatures: Committees of Congress* (Amherst: University of Massachusetts Press, 1970); Richard J. Fenno, Jr., *Congressmen in Committees* (Boston: Little, Brown, 1973); Steven S. Smith and Christopher J. Deering. *Committees in Congress* (Washington, D.C.: Congressional Quarterly Press, 1990).

2. There is one article devoted to the topic, Arthur T. Johnson, "Congress and Professional Sports, 1951–1978," *Annals of the American Academy of Political and Social Science* 445 (September 1979), 102–15.

3. Ibid.; Arthur T. Johnson and James H. Frey, eds., *Government and Sport: The Public Policy Issues* (Totowa, NJ: Rowman & Allanheld, 1985).

4. For a general treatment of boxing, see Jeffrey T. Sammons, *Beyond the Ring: The Role of Boxing in American Society* (Urbana: University of Illinois Press, 1988).

5. For histories of baseball, see Charles C. Alexander, *Our Game: An American Baseball History* (New York: Henry Holt, 1991); Harold Seymour, *Baseball* , 3 vols. (New York: Oxford University Press); David Q. Voigt, *American Baseball*, 3 vols. (University Park: Pennsylvania State University Press). For baseball's unique stature as the American game, see Allen Guttmann *From Ritual to Record: The Nature of Modern Sports* (New York: Columbia University Press, 1978).

6. For the marriage of professional football to network television, see Ron Powers, *Supertube: The Rise of Television Sports* (New York: Coward-McCann, 1984); Jim Spence and Dave Diles, *Up Close and Personal: The Inside Story of Network Television Sports* (New York: Atheneum, 1988); Bert Randolph Sugar, *The Thrill of Victory: The Inside Story of ABC Sports* (New York: Hawthorne Books, 1978). For a general treatment of professional football, see David Harris, *The League: The Rise and Fall of the NFL* (New York: Bantam Books, 1986).

7. For a history of basketball, see Glenn Dickey, *The History of Professional Basketball since 1896* (New York: Stein and Day, 1982).

Chapter 1

1. *New York Times*, 10 October 1905, 1; *Washington Post* 10 October 1905.

2. *New York Times*, 10 October 1905, 1.

3. *Washington Post*, 10 October 1905.

4. *New York Times*, 10 October 1905, 1.

5. Charles C. Alexander, *Our Game: An American Baseball History* (New York: Henry Holt, 1991), 142–43.

6. Eugene C. Murdock, *Ban Johnson: Czar of Baseball* (Westport: Greenwood Press, 1982), 208–09.

7. *Chicago Tribune*, 3 October 1924; *New York Times*, 3 October 1924, 1.

8. Murdock, *Ban Johnson*, 209.

9. Arthur Ruhl, "The Fight in the Desert," *Collier's* 45 (July 1910), 12–13.

10. Randy Roberts, *Papa Jack: Jack Johnson and the Era of White Hopes* (New York: Free Press; London: Collier Macmillan, 1983), 109.

11. Jeffrey T. Sammons *Beyond the Ring: The Role of Boxing in American Society* (Chicago: University of Illinois Press, 1988), 41.

12. Committee on Interstate and Foreign Commerce, United States House of Representatives, 61st Cong., 1st–2d sess. (1910–11), *Prohibition of Interstate Transportation of Pictures and Descriptions of Prizefights and the Nullification of State Anti-Gambling Laws*, 3.

13. Ibid., testimony of "Battling" Nelson, 4; *New York Times*, 18 May 1910, 8.

14. *Prohibition of Interstate Transportation of Pictures and Descriptions of Prizefights*, Nelson testimony, 8.

15. Roberts, *Papa Jack*, 135.

16. *Congressional Record*, 62d Cong. 2d sess., 48 (15 June 1912), 8236.

17. Ibid. (1 July 1912), 8551.

18. Roberts, *Papa Jack*, 135.

19. *Congressional Record*, 62d Cong., 2d sess., 48 (19 July 1912), 9305.

20. Ibid. (19 July 1912), 9307.

21. Roberts, *Papa Jack*, 137.

22. Ibid., 145.

23. Ibid., 161.

24. *Congressional Record*, 68th Cong., 1st sess., 65 (5 March 1924), 3601; Sammons, *Beyond the Ring*, 45.

25. Sammons, *Beyond the Ring*, 119.

26. *New York Times*, 9 April 1939, IV, 1.

27. Committee on Interstate Commerce, United States Senate, 76th Cong., 1st sess. (1939), *Legalizing Transportation of Prize-Fight Films*, testimony of Jack Dempsey, 7.

28. Ibid., 41.

29. *Washington Post*, 26 May 1939.

30. *Legalizing Transportation of Prize-Fight Films*, Dempsey testimony, 7; *Chicago Tribune*, 26 May 1939; *Washington Post*, 26 May 1939.

31. *Legalizing Transportation of Prize-Fight Films*, testimony of Neville Miller, 21.

32. Ibid., 43.

33. *Legalizing Transportation of Prize-Fight Films*, Dempsey testimony, 10.

34. Randy Roberts, *Jack Dempsey: The Manassa Mauler* (Baton Rouge: Louisiana State University Press, 1979), 267.

35. *Legalizing Transportation of Prize-Fight Films*, testimony of Fred J. Saddy, 54.

36. Roberts, *Papa Jack*, 224; Chris Mead, *Champion Joe Louis: Black Hero in White America* (New York: Charles Scribner's Sons, 1985).

37. Joe Louis, *My Life Story* (New York: Duell, Sloan and Pierce, 1947), 105.

38. Committee on Interstate Commerce, United States Senate, 76th Cong., 1st sess. (1939), *Divesting Prize-Fight Films of Their Interstate Character, Report*.

39. *Congressional Record*, 76th Cong., 1st sess., 84 (13 June 1939), 7084; Ibid., 2d sess., 86 (21 June 1940), 8898; Ibid. (3 July 1940), 9202.

Chapter 2

1. See George Goodwin, Jr., *The Little Legislatures: Committees of Congress* (Amherst: University of Massachusetts Press, 1970), 19; Steven S. Smith and Christopher J. Deering, *Committees in Congress* (Washington, D.C.: Congressional Quarterly Press, 1990), 28; William L. Morrow, *Congressional Committees* (New York: Charles Scribner's Sons, 1969), 39.

2. Smith and Deering, *Committees in Congress*, 43.

3. Morrow, *Congressional Committees*, 39.

4. Smith and Deering, *Committees in Congress*, 119–20; Morrow, *Congressional Committees*, 45.

5. Lynette P. Perkins, "Member Recruitment to a Mixed Goal Committee: The House Judiciary Committee," *Journal of Politics*, 43 (May 1981), 349–64.

6. Ibid., 360–61.

7. Peter H. Schuck, *The Judiciary Committees* (New York: Grossman, 1975), 92; Morrow, *Congressional Committees*, 40; see also Smith and Deering, *Committees in Congress*, 42.

8. Smith and Deering, *Committees in Congress*, 40.

9. Ibid., 40–41; Goodwin, *The Little Legislatures,* 164; Morrow, *Congressional Committees*, 32.

10. Emanuel Celler, *You Never Leave Brooklyn: The Autobiography of Emanuel Celler* (New York: John Day, 1953), 165.

11. Celler saved a few letters he received from disgruntled players, after the investigation, but none that he may have received before the investigation.

12. Celler, *You Never Leave Brooklyn*, 167.

13. James B. Dworkin, *Owners Versus Players: Baseball and Collective Bargaining* (Boston: Auburn House, 1981), 57; Lionel S. Sobel, *Professional Sports and the Law* (New York: Law-Arts, 1977), 7; Randy Roberts and James S. Olson, *Winning Is the Only Thing: Sports in America Since 1945* (Baltimore: Johns Hopkins University Press, 1989), 48.

14. *Gardella v. Chandler*, 79 F. Supp. 260 (1948).

15. *Sporting News*, 4 July 1951.

16. Ibid., 25 July 1951; *Washington Post*, 19 July 1951.

17. *Sporting News*, 1 August 1951.

18. Ibid., 25 July 1951.

19. Minutes of Meeting of Subcommittee on Study of Monopoly Power, 19 September 1951, Emanuel Celler Papers, Library of Congress, Washington, D.C. (hereafter cited as ECP).

20. Ibid, 26 July 1951.

21. Subcommittee on the Study of Monopoly Power, United States House of Representatives, 82d Cong., 1st sess. (1951), *Study of Monopoly Power: Organized Baseball, Part 6, Hearings*, testimony of Ty Cobb, 15; *Washington Post*, 31 July 1951.

22. James B. Dworkin, "Balancing the Rights of Professional Athletes and Team Owners: The Proper Role of Government," in Arthur T. Johnson and James H. Frey, eds., *Government and Sport: The Public Policy Issues* (Totowa, NJ: Rowman & Allanheld, 1985), 22; Harold Seymour, *Baseball*, 3 vols. (New York: Oxford University Press, 1960), vol. 1 *The Early Years*, 111–12.

23. *Study of Monopoly Power: Organized Baseball, Part 6, Hearings,* 15.

24. *New York Times*, 3 July 1951, 1; *Study of Monopoly Power: Organized Baseball, Part 6, Hearings*, 23.

25. Charles C. Alexander, *Ty Cobb* (New York: Oxford University Press, 1984), 236–40; Ty Cobb, *My Life in Baseball: The True Record* (New York: Doubleday, 1961), 273.

26. *Sporting News*, 8 August 1951; *Washington Post*, 31 July 1951.

27. *Sporting News*, 8 August 1951.

28. Ibid.; *Washington Post*, 2 August 1951.

29. *Study of Monopoly Power: Organized Baseball, Part 6, Hearings*, testimony of Ford Frick, 86.

30. *Sporting News*, 8 August 1951.

31. *Study of Monopoly Power: Organized Baseball, Part 6, Hearings*, Frick testimony, 1054.

32. Ibid., 40, 84; *Sporting News*, 8 August 1951; *New York Times*, 31 July 1951, 1.

33. *Study of Monopoly Power: Organized Baseball, Part 6, Hearings*, Frick testimony, 25.

34. *Sporting News*, 4 July 1951.

35. *New York Times*, 7 August 1951, 1; *Washington Post*, 7 August 1951.

36. *Study of Monopoly Power: Organized Baseball, Part 6, Hearings*, testimony of A.B. Chandler, 287.

37. Ibid., 258–60; *Sporting News*, 15 August 1951.

38. *Study of Monopoly Power: Organized Baseball, Part 6, Hearings*, testimony of Fred Hutchinson, 846; *Sporting News*, 11 July 1951.

39. *Study of Monopoly Power: Organized Baseball, Part 6, Hearings*, testimony of Pee Wee Reese, 853; testimony of Louis Boudreau, 859.

40. Baseball Notes, ECP.

41. Moore was suggesting that owners do what they did in 1987; that is, conspire to hold down salaries. In 1988, however, a federal arbitrator sided with the Major League Baseball Players Association and forced owners to compensate certain players hurt by their actions, including Kirk Gibson, Tim Raines, and Bob Horner.

42. *Study of Monopoly Power: Organized Baseball Part 6, Hearings*, testimony of Francis Moore, 916.

43. *Sporting News*, 17 October 1951.

44. *Study of Monopoly Power: Organized Baseball, Part 6, Hearings*, testimony of Frederick A. Johnson, 883.

45. Ibid., testimony of Ross Horning; *Sporting News*, 15 August 1951; *New York Times*, 8 August 1951, 6; "Baseball Faces Squeeze Play," *Business Week*, 11 August 1951, 23.

46. Letters to Emanuel Celler, 6–7 November 1951, ECP.

47. *Study of Monopoly Power: Organized Baseball, Part 6, Hearings,* testimony of Philip K. Wrigley, 735–38.

48. Minutes of Meeting of Subcommittee on Study of Monopoly Power, 25 July 1951, ECP.

49. *Sporting News,* 8 August 1951; *New York Times,* 3 August 1951, 5; *Washington Post,* 3 August 1951.

50. *Sporting News,* 22 August 1951.

51. Ibid., 15 August 1951.

52. Ibid., 31 October 1951.

53. Subcommittee on the Study of Monopoly Power, United States House of Representatives, 82d Cong., 2d sess. (1952), *Organized Baseball, Report,* 232.

54. Lee Lowenfish and Tony Lupien, *The Imperfect Diamond* (New York: Stein and Day 1980), 181.

55. David B. Truman, *The Governmental Process* (New York: Alfred A. Knopf, 1963), 373.

56. Ibid., 372.

57. Morrow, *Congressional Committees,* 92.

58. Quoted in Goodwin, *The Little Legislatures,* 164.

59. Estes Kefauver and Jack Levin, *A Twentieth Century Congress* (New York: Greenwood Press, 1969), 13.

60. James Hamilton, *The Power to Probe: A Study of Congressional Investigations* (New York: Random House, 1976), xii.

61. Smith and Deering, *Committees in Congress,* 1.

62. Goodwin, *The Little Legislatures,* 173.

63. Ibid.

64. Woodrow Wilson, *Congressional Government: A Study in American Politics* (New York: World, 1956), 63.

65. *Sporting News,* 28 May 1952.

66. Letter from Ford Frick to Emanuel Celler, 28 May 1952, ECP.

67. *New York Times,* 27 May 1952, 3.

68. Letter from "A Busted Minor Leaguer" to Emanuel Celler, 26 February 1953, ECP.

69. "Shape of Things," *Nation,* 173 (August 1951) 103.

Chapter 3

1. "Are Ballplayers Slaves?" *U.S. News and World Report,* 31 (August 1951), 21.

2. *Sporting News,* 19 June 1957.

3. *Toolson v. New York Yankees, Inc.* 346 U.S. 356 (1953).

4. *U.S. v. International Boxing Club* 348 U.S. 236 (1955).

5. *Radovich v. National Football League* 352 U.S. 200 (1957).

6. Subcommittee on Anti-Trust and Monopoly, United States House of Representatives, 85th Cong., 1st sess. (1957), *Organized Professional Team Sports, Hearings,* 2.

7. Warren Freedman, *Professional Sports and Anti-Trust* (New York: Quorum Books, 1987), 4.

8. *Sporting News,* 19 June 1957; *Washington Post,* December 23, 1959.

9. House, *Organized Professional Team Sports, Hearings,* 7; *Congressional Record,* 85th Cong. 2d sess. 104 (24 June 1958), 12103.

10. House, *Organized Professional Team Sports, Hearings,* testimony of Ford Frick, 91; *Sporting News,* 26 June 1957.

11. House, *Organized Professional Team Sports, Hearings,* testimony of Walter O'Malley; *Sporting News,* 3 July 1957; Neil J. Sullivan, *The Dodgers Move West* (New York: Oxford University Press, 1987), 122.

12. House, *Organized Professional Team Sports, Hearings,* testimony of Bob Feller, 172; *Sporting News,* 3 July 1957; *Washington Post,* 26 June 1957.

13. *Sporting News,* 3 July 1957.

14. Ibid., 17 July 1957; *Washington Post,* 12 July 1957.

15. Lee Lowenfish and Tony Lupien, *The Imperfect Diamond* (New York: Stein and Day, 1980), 158.

16. House, *Organized Professional Team Sports, Hearings,* testimony of Stan Musial, 1305; *New York Times,* 26 June 1957, 1.

17. Joe Garagiola to Kenneth B. Keating, 11 September 1957, Kenneth B. Keating Papers, Rush Rhees Library, University of Rochester, Rochester, NY (hereafter cited as KKP).

18. House, *Organized Professional Team Sports, Hearings,* testimony of Bert Bell, 2498.

19. House, *Organized Professional Team Sports, Hearings,* testimony of Clarence Campbell, 2995.

20. *Congressional Record,* 85th Cong., 2d sess., 104 (June 24, 1958), 12103; *Sporting News,* 2 July 1958.

21. Press Release, 23 June 1958, KKP.

22. *Sporting News,* 2 July 1958.

23. *Sporting News,* 2 July 1958.

24. Joseph Bruce Gorman, *Estes Kefauver: A Political Biography* (New York: Oxford University Press, 1971), 27–28; see also Charles Fonteney, *Estes Kefauver: A Biography* (Knoxville: University of Tennessee Press, 1980); Jack Anderson and Fred Blumenthal, *The Kefauver Story* (New York: Dial Press, 1956).

25. *Sporting News,* 9 July 1958.

26. Subcommittee on Anti-Trust and Monopoly, United States Senate, 85th Cong., 2d sess. (1958), *Organized Professional Team Sports, Hearings*, 2; *Sporting News*, 9 July 1958.

27. Senate, *Organized Professional Team Sports, Hearings*, 25, 380.

28. Robert W. Creamer, *Stengel: His Life and Times* (New York: Simon and Schuster, 1984), 276.

29. Senate, *Organized Professional Team Sports, Hearings*, testimony of Casey Stengel, 13.

30. *Sporting News*, 16 July 1958.

31. Creamer, *Stengel*, 278–79.

32. Senate, *Organized Professional Team Sports, Hearings*, testimony of Mickey Mantle, 24.

33. Ibid., testimony of Ted Williams, 31; *Sporting News*, 16 July 1958. See also Michael Seidel, *Ted Williams: A Baseball Life* (Chicago: Contemporary Books, 1991), 309.

34. Senate, *Organized Professional Team Sports, Hearings*, testimony of Stan Musial, 35.

35. *Sporting News*, 16 July 1958.

36. Senate, *Organized Professional Team Sports, Hearings*, testimony of Bob Feller, 305.

37. Ibid., testimony of Jackie Robinson, 296.

38. Ibid., testimony of Bert Bell, 404.

39. Ibid., testimony of William Howerton, 328.

40. Estes Kefauver to Ernest Barcella, 7 August 1958, Estes Kefauver Papers, Special Collections, Hoskins Library, University of Tennessee, Knoxville, TN (hereafter cited as EKP).

41. Estes Kefauver to Kenneth B. Keating, 16 January 1959, KKP.

42. *Sporting News*, 5 August 1959.

43. Subcommittee on Anti-Trust and Monopoly, United States Senate, 86th Cong., 1st sess. (1959), *Organized Professional Team Sports, 1959, Hearings Before Subcommittee on Anti-Trust and Monopoly*, 3.

44. Nashville *Banner*, 4 February 1959, clipping in EKP.

45. *Organized Professional Team Sports, 1959, Hearings*, 11.

46. Ibid., testimony of Ford Frick, 52; *New York Times*, 30 July 1959, 32.

47. *Sporting News*, 12 August 1959.

48. *Organized Professional Team Sports, 1959, Hearings*, testimony of Branch Rickey, 152.

49. Ibid., testimony of Bert Bell, 30.

50. Ibid., testimony of Maurice Podoloff, 196.

51. *Sporting News*, 29 July 1959.

52. Ibid., 5 August 1959.

53. Ibid., 29 July 1959.

54. Ibid., 26 August 1959.

55. Ibid., 11, 18 May 1960.

56. Subcommittee on Anti-Trust and Monopoly, United States Senate, 86th Cong. 2d sess. (1960), *Organized Professional Team Sports, 1960, Hearings*, testimony of Branch Rickey, 65; see also Lance E. Davis, "Self-Regulation in Baseball," in Roger G. Noll, ed., *Government and the Sports Business* (Washington, D.C.: Brookings Institution, 1974), 367.

57. *Organized Professional Team Sports, 1960, Hearings*, testimony of Branch Rickey, 79.

58. Ibid., 66.

59. Ibid.; Branch Rickey to Philip Hart, 20 June 1960, Philip Hart Papers, Bentley Historical Library, University of Michigan, Ann Arbor, MI (hereafter cited as PHP).

60. Attendance at minor league games had dropped from 42 million in 1949 to 15 million in 1957. See Benjamin G. Rader, *In Its Own Image: How Television Has Transformed Sports* (New York: Free Press, 1984), 59.

61. *Organized Professional Team Sports, 1960, Hearings*, testimony of Ford Frick, 104.

62. *Sporting News*, 25 May 1960.

63. *Organized Professional Team Sports, 1960, Hearings*, testimony of Ford Frick, 104.

64. See numerous letters sent by minor league officials in the KKP and PHP.

65. Branch Rickey to Philip Hart, 20 June 1960; William Shea to Philip Hart, 21 June 1960, PHP; *Sporting News*, 22 June 1960; Martin Enright to Kenneth B. Keating, 9 June 1960, KKP.

66. *Sporting News*, 15 June 1960.

67. Ibid., 22 June 1960.

68. Ibid., 6 July 1960; *New York Times*, 29 June 1960, 36.

69. Ford Frick to Philip Hart, 30 June 1960, PHP; *Sporting News*, 6 July 1960.

70. *Sporting News*, 6 July 1960.

71. Ibid., 20 July 1960.

72. Edwin C. Johnson to Estes Kefauver, 20 May 1961 EKP; *Sporting News*, 10 August 1960.

Chapter 4

1. See Joseph Bruce Gorman, *Estes Kefauver: A Political Biography* (New York: Oxford University Press, 1971), 369; and Charles L. Fontenay, *Estes Kefauver: A Biography* (Knoxville: University of Tennessee Press, 1980).

2. Peter H. Schuck, *The Judiciary Committees* (New York: Grossman, 1975), 69; *Sporting News*, 13 March 1965.

3. Subcommittee on Anti-Trust and Monopoly, United States Senate, 88th Cong., 2d sess. (1964), *Professional Sports Anti-Trust Bill, 1964, Hearings*, 1.

4. Ibid., 3.

5. Ibid., testimony of Ford Frick, 12.

6. Ibid., testimony of Bob Allison, 37.

7. Ibid., Frick testimony, 12; *Washington Post*, 31 January 1964.

8. *Professional Sports Anti-Trust Bill, 1964, Hearings*, testimony of Pete Rozelle, 111; *Washington Post*, 18 February 1964.

9. *Professional Sports Anti-Trust Bill, 1964, Hearings*, testimony of Ordell Braase, 97; *Washington Post*, 18 February 1964.

10. *Professional Sports Anti-Trust Bill, 1964, Hearings*, testimony of Walter Kennedy, 53; testimony of Clarence Campbell, 61.

11. Roger Kahn, "The Yankees: Descent from Olympus," *Saturday Evening Post*, 237 (September 1964), 80–83; "Television Tilts the Old Ballgame," *Life*, 57 (August 1964), 87–88; David Q. Voigt, *American Baseball*, 3 vols. (University Park, Pennsylvania State University Press) 1983), vol. 3: *From Post-War Expansion to the Electronic Age*, 319.

12. Subcommittee on Anti-Trust and Monopoly, United States Senate, 89th Cong., 1st sess. (1965), *Professional Sports Anti-Trust Bill, 1965, Hearings*, 2.

13. Ibid., testimony of Frank Stanton, 6.

14. Ibid., testimony of Ford Frick, 38; *New York Times*, 20 February 1965, 3.

15. *Professional Sports Anti-Trust Bill, 1965, Hearings*, testimony of Joe Cronin, 73.

16. *Washington Post*, 19 February 1964; *Sporting News*, 29 February 1964.

17. *Professional Sports Anti-Trust Bill, 1964, Hearings*, testimony of Charles Finley, 113.

18. Ibid., testimony of Walter Kennedy, 22; testimony of Pete Rozelle, 198; testimony of Clarence Campbell; 222.

19. Ibid., testimony of Thomas Moore, 77; testimony of Julian Goodman, 89; *New York Times*, 24 February 1965, 4.

20. *Congressional Record*, 89th Cong. 1st sess., 111 (21 August 1965), 22329.

21. *Flood v. Kuhn*, 407 U.S. 258 (1972); Lionel S. Sobel, *Professional Sports and the Law* (New York: Law-Arts Publishers, Inc., 1977), 57.

22. *New York Times*, 17 June 1972, 23.

23. Committee on Commerce, United States Senate, 92d Cong., 2d sess. (1972), *Federal Sports Act of 1972, Hearings,* testimony of Bowie Kuhn, 178; *Washington Post,* 24 June 1972.

24. *Federal Sports Act of 1972, Hearings,* testimony of Pete Rozelle, 136.

25. Ibid., testimony of Walter Kennedy, 211.

26. Ibid., testimony of Howard Cosell; *Washington Post,* 20 February 1972; *New York Times,* 20 February 1972, 48; Howard Cosell, *Like It Is* (Chicago: Playboy Press, 1974), 131–34.

27. See James B. Dworkin, *Owners Versus Players: Baseball and Collective Bargaining* (Boston: Auburn House 1981); Lee Lowenfish and Tony Lupien, *The Imperfect Diamond* (New York: Stein and Day, 1980); Robert C. Berry et al., *Labor Relations in Professional Sports* (Dover: Auburn House, 1986).

28. Dworkin, *Owners Versus Players,* 83.

29. *Kapp v. National Football League,* 390 F. Supp. 73 (1974).

30. Committee on Judiciary, United States House of Representatives, 94th Cong., 1st sess. (1975), *Rights of Professional Athletes,* testimony of Emanuel Celler, 9; *New York Times,* 15 October 1975, 28; *Washington Post,* 15 October 1975.

31. For a discussion of the role and rights of special or select congressional committees, see Steven S. Smith and Christopher J. Deering *Committees in Congress* (Washington, D.C.: Congressional Quarterly Press, 1990), 4–6; David B. Truman, *The Governmental Process* (New York: Alfred A. Knopf, 1963), 379.

32. Select Committee on Professional Sports, United States House of Representatives, 94 Congress, 2 session (1976), *Inquiry into Professional Sports, Part 1,* 2.

33. Ibid., testimony of Bowie Kuhn, 27.

34. *Washington Post,* 22 July 1976.

35. Select Committee on Professional Sports, United States House of Representatives, 94 Congress, 2 session (1976), *Inquiry into Professional Sports, Part 2,* testimony of M. Donald Grant, 384; *New York Times,* 22 September 1976, 33.

36. *Inquiry into Professional Sports, Part 1,* testimony of Richard Dozer, 556.

37. *Inquiry into Professional Sports, Part 1,* testimony of James Michener, 92; *Washington Post,* 15 September 1976.

38. *Inquiry into Professional Sports, Part 1,* testimony of Pete Rozelle, 78; testimony of Clarence Campbell, 172; testimony of Lawrence O'Brien, 613.

39. Ibid., testimony of Marvin Miller, 367; *Washington Post,* 3 August, 23 July 1976.

40. *Inquiry into Professional Sports, Part 1*, testimony of Edward Garvey, 215.

41. Ibid., testimony of Howard Cosell, 583; *Washington Post*, 23 August 1976.

42. Select Committee on Professional Sports, United States House of Representatives, 94th Cong., 2d sess. (1976–77), *Inquiry into Professional Sports: Final Meetings*, 15.

43. *Washington Post*, 22 July 1976.

44. Committee on Judiciary, United States House of Representatives, 97 Congress, 1st–2d sess. (1981–82), *Anti-Trust Laws and Professional Sports*, testimony of Bowie Kuhn, 427; *Washington Post*, 5 February 1982.

45. *Anti-Trust Laws and Professional Sports*, testimony of Marvin Miller; *New York Times*, 25 February 1982, II, 20.

46. *Washington Post*, 11 December 1992, 3; *USA Today*, 10–11 December 1992.

47. Dworkin, *Owners Versus Players*, 71.

Chapter 5

1. *Congressional Record*, 60th Cong. 2d sess., 86 (9 April 1940), 4230.

2. *United States v. International Boxing Club*, 348 U.S. 236 (January 1955).

3. Jeffrey T. Sammons, *Beyond the Ring: The Role of Boxing in American Society* (Chicago: University of Illinois Press, 1988), 163. See also, Barney Nagler, *James Norris and the Decline of Boxing* (Indianapolis: Bobbs-Merrill, 1964).

4. Subcommittee on Anti-Trust and Monopoly, United States Senate, 86th Cong., 2 sess. (1960), *Professional Boxing, Part 1: Jacob "Jake" LaMotta*, 1–2; Speech to the floor of the Senate, 26 August 1956, Estes Kefauver Papers, Special Collections, Hoskins Library, University of Tennessee, Knoxville, TN (hereafter cited as EKP).

5. *New York Times*, 16 June 1960, 42.

6. Jack Anderson and Fred Blumenthal, *The Kefauver Story* (New York: Dial Press, 1956), 139.

7. Joseph Bruce Gorman, *Estes Kefauver: A Political Biography* (New York: Oxford University Press, 1971), 102; Ronald Gray, *Congressional Television: A Legislative History* (Westport, CT: Greenwood Press, 1984), 37.

8. Chattanooga *Free Press*, 2 September 1959, clipping in EKP.

9. Charles L. Fontenay, *Estes Kefauver: A Biography* (Knoxville: University of Tennessee Press, 1980), 287–88.

10. *Professional Boxing, Part 1*, 3.

11. Nagler, *James Norris and the Decline of Boxing*, 227. For a discussion of the role of the congressional special investigator, see George Goodwin, *The Little Legislatures: Committees of Congress* (Amherst: University of Massachusetts Press, 1970), 165.

12. Sammons, *Beyond the Ring*, passim.; Nagler, *James Norris and the Decline of Boxing*, passim.

13. *Professional Boxing, Part 1*, testimony of Jacob LaMotta, 7, 26; *Washington Post*, 15 June 1960.

14. *Professional Boxing, Part 1*, LaMotta testimony, 31.

15. Ibid., 37.

16. Letter from Jake LaMotta to Philip Hart, 16 March 1961, Philip Hart Papers, Bentley Historical Library, University of Michigan, Ann Arbor, MI (hereafter cited as PHP.)

17. Sammons, *Beyond the Ring*, 148.

18. *Professional Boxing, Part 1*, testimony of Joseph LaMotta, 50.

19. "Heads, Not Headlines," *Sports Illustrated*, 13 (5 December 1960), 12.

20. Subcommittee on Anti-Trust and Monopoly, United States Senate, 86th Cong., 2d sess. (1960), *Professional Boxing, Part 2: Frank Carbo*, 269.

21. Ibid., 272.

22. Memorandum from John Bonomi to Estes Kefauver, EKP; *New York Times*, 9 December 1960, 40; *Washington Post*, 9 December 1960.

23. Gilbert Rogin, "Norris' Last Stand," *Sports Illustrated*, 13 (19 December 1960), 12–15.

24. Sammons, *Beyond the Ring*, 138.

25. *Professional Boxing, Part 2*, testimony of James Norris, 549; *New York Times*, 9–10 December 1960, 40, 17; *Washington Post*, 9–10 December 1960; Rogin, "Norris' Last Stand."

26. Sammons, *Beyond the Ring*, 152.

27. *Professional Boxing, Part 2*, testimony of Truman Gibson, 331; *New York Times*, 6 December 1960, 1; *Washington Post*, 7 December 1960.

28. "Only One Thing to Say," *Newsweek*, 56 (26 December 1960), 37.

29. "Mr. Gray's Eminence" Ibid., 19 December 1960, 64.

30. *Professional Boxing, Part 2*, testimony of Frank Carbo, 836; *New York Times*, 14 December 1960, 54; *Washington Post*, 15 December 1960.

31. Sammons, *Beyond the Ring*, 167.

32. *Professional Boxing, Part 2*, testimony of Sonny Liston, 758; *New York Times*, 14 December 1960, 54; *Washington Post*, 13 December 1960; Martin Kane, "Estes vs. The Hoods," *Sports Illustrated*, 13 (26 December 1960), 28.

33. *Washington Post*, 15 December 1960.

34. Subcommittee on Anti-Trust and Monopoly, United States Senate, 87th Cong. 1st sess. (1961), *Professional Boxing, Part 3*, statement of Clair Engle, 1260.

35. *Professional Boxing, Part 3*, testimony of Rocky Marciano, 1265; *Washington Post*, 1 June 1961.

36. *Professional Boxing, Part 3*, testimony of Jack Dempsey, 1404.

37. *Washington Post*, 22 April 1961.

38. *Professional Boxing, Part 3*, testimony of Gene Tunney, 1422.

39. *Washington Post*, 2 June 1961.

40. *Professional Boxing, Part 3*, testimony of Joe Louis, 1330.

41. Ibid., testimony of Melvin Krulewitch, 1339.

42. Ibid., testimony of Harry Falk, 1305.

43. Ibid., testimony of Nat Fleischer, 1440; testimony of Alfred Klein, 1357.

44. Letter from Estes Kefauver to Robert F. Kennedy, 8 March 1961, EKP.

45. *New York Times*, 30 March 1961, 34.

46. Hans J. Massaquoi, "Should Boxing Be Abolished?" *Ebony*, 17 (June 1962), 44–46.

47. "Brinkley vs. the Brontosaurus," *Sports Illustrated*, 20 (4 May 1964), 16.

48. Ibid.

49. Subcommittee on Anti-Trust and Monopoly, United States Senate, 88th Cong., 2d sess. (1964) *Professional Boxing, Part 4: Liston-Clay Fight*, 1845; Wilfrid Sheed, *Muhammad Ali* (New York: Thomas Y. Crowell, 1975), 42.

50. *Professional Boxing, Part 4*, 1846.

51. Ibid., 1597.

52. Sheed, *Muhammad Ali*, 42.

53. *Professional Boxing, Part 4*, testimony of Gordon Davidson, 1687.

54. Ibid., statement of Thruston Morton, 1691.

55. Ibid., testimony of Gordon Davidson, 1687; *Washington Post*, 27 March 1964.

56. *Professional Boxing, Part 4*, testimony of Jack Nilon, 1657; *New York Times*, 26 March 1964, 44.

57. *Professional Boxing, Part 4*, Margolis testimony; *New York Times*, 26 March 1964, 44; "My Co-operation," *Newsweek*, 63 (6 April 1964), 60; Robert H. Boyle, "Taking Stock of Sonny," *Sports Illustrated*, 20 (6 April 1964), 24–27.

58. *Professional Boxing, Part 4*, testimony of Sam Margolis, *Washington Post*, 31 March 1964.

59. *Professional Boxing, Part 4*, testimony of Robert Nilon; *New York Times*, 31 March 1964, 42.

60. Letter from Melvin Krulewitch to Kenneth Keating, 13 August 1963, Kenneth Keating Papers, Rush Rhees Library, University of Rochester, Rochester, NY (hereafter cited as KKP.)

61. Letters re boxing bill, April–May, 1964, PHP.

62. Memorandum from Cecil Mackey to Philip Hart, 17 September 1963, PHP.

63. Letter from Philip Hart to Robert F. Kennedy, 17 March 1964, PHP.

64. Committee on Judiciary, United States Senate, 87th Cong., 2d sess. (1962), *Bribery in Sports Contests*; Committee on Judiciary, United States Senate, 88th Cong., 1st sess. (1963), *Bribery in Sports Contests;* Committee on Judiciary, United States House of Representatives, 88th Cong., 1st sess. (1963) *Bribery in Sports Contests.*

65. James H. Frey, "Gambling, Sports, and Public Policy," in Arthur T. Johnson and James H. Frey, eds., *Government and Sport: The Public Policy Issues* (Totowa, NJ: Rowman & Allanheld, 1985), 209.

66. "Theater of the Absurd," *Time*, 85 (4 June 1965), 68–69.

67. Howard Cosell, *Cosell* (Chicago: Playboy Press, 1973), 181.

68. "The True Picture," *Sports Illustrated*, 72 (7 June 1965), 12.

69. "Theater of the Absurd," 68–69.

70. *Congressional Quarterly*, 6 August 1965, 1581.

71. Committee on Interstate and Foreign Commerce, United States House of Representatives, 89th Cong., 1st sess. (1965), *Federal Boxing Commission, Hearings*, 2.

72. Ibid., 8.

73. Letter from Emanuel Celler to Julius Helfand, 3 June 1965, Emanuel Celler Papers, Library of Congress, Washington, D.C. (hereafter cited as ECP.)

74. *Washington Post*, 7 July 1965.

75. *Federal Boxing Commission, Hearings*, testimony of Jack Dempsey, 25.

76. Ibid., testimony of Gene Tunney, 43; *New York Times*, 7 July 1965, 28.

77. *Federal Boxing Commission, Hearings*, testimony of Rocky Marciano, 61.

78. Ibid., testimony of Nat Fleischer, 120; *Washington Post*, 8 July 1965.

79. *Federal Boxing Commission, Hearings*, testimony of Melvin Krulewitch, 109.

80. Ibid., testimony of Arch Hindeman, 164.

81. Ibid., testimony of William Reitzer; *Washington Post*, 9 July 1965.
82. Ibid., 32.
83. *Congressional Record*, 89th Cong. 1st sess., 111 (16 August 1965), 20471.
84. *Congressional Quarterly*, August 16, 1965, 1645.
85. "Big Week for Boxing," *Sports Illustrated*, 23 (30 August 1965), 7.
86. *Congressional Quarterly*, 14 April 1979, 703; *Washington Post*, 29 March 1979.
87. Committee on Education and Labor, United States House of Representatives, 90th Cong., 1st sess. (1979), *Hearings on the Creation of a Federal Boxing Board,* 81; *New York Times*, 30 March 1979, II, 6.
88. *Hearings on the Creation of a Federal Boxing Board*, testimony of Howard Cosell, 137; *Washington Post*, 4 April 1979.
89. Ibid., testimony of Jersey Joe Walcott, 112.
90. *Hearings on the Creation of a Federal Boxing Board,* testimony of Don King, 64; *Washington Post,* 3 March 1979; *New York Times*, 3 March 1979, II, 6.
91. Committee on Energy and Commerce, United States House of Representatives, 98th Cong., 1st sess. (1983), *Boxing Reform, Hearings*, testimony of Floyd Patterson, 16; *New York Times*, 16 February 1983, 26; *USA Today*, 16 February 1983.
92. George Lundberg, "Boxing Should Be Banned in Civilized Societies," *Journal of the American Medical Association,* 249 (14 January 1983), 250.
93. *Boxing Reform, Hearings*, testimony of Howard Cosell, 4; *USA Today*, 16 February 1983; *Washington Post*, 16 February 1983.
94. *Boxing Reform, Hearings*, testimony of Donald Fraser, 98.
95. Ibid., testimony of Bert Sugar, 214.
96. *Congressional Record*, 98th Cong., 1st sess., 130 (30 July 1983), 1591.
97. *Congressional Quarterly*, 5 August 1965, 1582.
98. *Professional Boxing, Part 3,* 1325.

Chapter 6

1. Benjamin G. Rader, *In Its Own Image; How Television Has Transformed Sports* (New York: Macmillan, 1984), 59.
2. Committee on Interstate and Foreign Commerce, United States Senate, 83d Cong., 1st sess. (1953), *Broadcasting and Telecasting Baseball Games: Hearings on S. 1396,* 5; Committee on Interstate and Foreign Commerce, United States Senate, 83d Cong., 1st sess. (1953), *Report from Committee on Judiciary and Foreign Commerce to accompany S. 1396,* 5.

3. "Bush League Baseball on the Rocks," *Business Week* (14 August 1954), 90.

4. *Report from Committee on Judiciary and Foreign Commerce to accompany S. 1396*, 4.

5. Ibid., 2.

6. *Broadcasting and Televising Baseball Games, Hearings*, 2.

7. Ibid., testimony of Ford Frick, 16.

8. Ibid., 17.

9. Ibid., testimony of George Trautman, 26.

10. Ibid., testimony of Warren Giles, 27.

11. Ibid., testimony of A.B. Chandler, 146–47.

12. *Sporting News*, 20 May 1953; *Broadcasting*, May 18, 1953, 46.

13. *Broadcasting and Televising Baseball Games, Hearings*, testimony of Gordon McLendon, 97–108; *New York Times*, 12 May 1953, 2.

14. Ibid.

15. *Washington Post*, 12 May 1953.

16. *Sporting News*, 11 June 1953.

17. *Congressional Record*, 83rd Cong., 1st sess., 99 (8 July 1953), 8201.

18. *Report to accompany S. 1396*, 12.

19. *Broadcasting*, 22 March 1954, 53.

20. *Congressional Record*, 83d Cong., 2d sess., 100 (23 February 1954), 8120.

21. Subcommittee on Anti-Trust and Monopoly, United States Senate, 83rd Cong., 2d sess. (1954), *Subjecting Professional Baseball Clubs to the Anti-Trust Laws: Hearings on S.J. Res. 133*, testimony of Ford Frick, 90; *Sporting News*, 14 April 1954.

22. *Subjecting Professional Baseball Clubs to the Anti-Trust Laws*, testimony of Stanley Barnes, 4.

23. Ibid.; testimony of Joe Garagiola, 42; *Sporting News*, 14 April 1954.

24. *Subjecting Professional Baseball Clubs to the Anti-Trust Laws*, testimony of August Busch, 95; *Sporting News*, 2 June 1954; *Broadcasting*, 31 May 1954, 52.

25. *Sporting News*, 2 June 1954.

26. Ibid., *Subjecting Professional Baseball Clubs to the Anti-Trust Laws*, 62.

27. *Broadcasting*, 31 May 1954, 52.

28. *Sporting News*, 17 March 1954.

29. Robert Obojski, *Bush League: A History of Minor League Baseball* (New York: Macmillan, 1975), 27.

30. Rader, *In Its Own Image*, 58; Ira Horowitz, "Sports Broadcasting," in Roger G. Noll, ed., *Government and the Sports Business* (Washington, D.C.: Brookings Institution, 1974), 279.

31. *United States v. National Football League*, 196 F. Supp. 445 (1961); *Broadcasting*, 31 July 1961, 60; *Sporting News*, 2 August 1961; *New York Times*, 22 July 1961, 45.

32. *Sporting News*, 23 August 1961.

33. *Broadcasting*, 21 August 1961, 52.

34. Ibid., 24 July 1961, 61.

35. Rader, *In Its Own Image*, 89.

36. *Broadcasting*, 24 July 1961, 61.

37. Subcommittee on Anti-Trust and Monopoly, United States House of Representatives, 87th Cong. 1st sess. (1961), *Telecasting of Professional Sports Contest, Hearings*, 5.

38. Ibid., 9; *Broadcasting*, 28 August 1961, 60.

39. *Telecasting of Professional Sports Contests, Hearings*, testimony of Ford Frick, 53; *Broadcasting*, 28 August 1961, 60.

40. *Telecasting of Professional Sports Contests, Hearings*, testimony of Vincent Wasilewski, 54; *Broadcasting*, 4 September 1961, 54.

41. *Broadcasting*, 4 September 1961, 54; Rader, *In Its Own Image*, 90.

42. Ibid., 90.

43. *Congressional Record*, 87th Cong., 1st sess. 107 (18, 21, 30 September 1961), 20059, 20662, 21212.

44. Letter from Estes Kefauver to Matty Brescia, 12 October 1961, Estes Kefauver Papers, Special Collections, Hoskins Library, University of Tennessee, Knoxville.

45. Committee on Judiciary, United States House of Representatives, 87th Cong., 1st sess. (1961), *Telecasting of Professional Sports Contests, Report on H.R. 9096*, 1.

46. Ibid., 4.

47. Letters from Clinton Hester to Philip Hart, 16 August, 5 September 1961, Philip Hart Papers, Bentley Historical Library, University of Michigan, Ann Arbor.

Chapter 7

1. Joan Chandler, *Television and National Sport: The United States and Great Britain* (Urbana: University of Illinois Press, 1988); Benjamin G. Rader, *American Sports: From the Age of Folk Games to the Age of Spectators* (Englewood Cliffs, NJ: Prentice-Hall, 1983), 242; William O. Johnson, "T.V. Made It All A New Ballgame," in John T. Talamini and

Charles H. Page, eds., *Sport and Society: An Anthology* (Boston: Little, Brown, 1973), 454–72.

2. Bert Randolph Sugar, *The Thrill of Victory: The Inside Story of ABC Sports* (New York: Hawthorne Books, 1978), 270; William Leggett, "The 28 Million-Dollar Deal," *Sports Illustrated*, 20 (3 February 1964), 16–17.

3. Benjamin G. Rader, *In Its Own Image: How Television Has Transformed Sports* (New York: Free Press, 1984), 92.

4. *U.S. v. National Football League* 116 F. Supp. 319 (1953).

5. "Bootleg T.V.," *Sports Illustrated*, 17 (12 November 1962), 6–8; "On the 50-Yard Line, 75 Miles from the Game," *Business Week* 5 January 1963, 24–25.

6. *Broadcasting*, 9 October 1972, 26; *Chicago Tribune*, 4 October 1972.

7. Committee on Communications, United States Senate, 92 Congress, 2 session (1972), *Blackout of Sporting Events on T.V.: Hearings*, 6.

8. Ibid., 7.

9. Ibid., testimony of Pete Rozelle, 64.

10. *New York Times*, 5 October 1972, 61.

11. *Blackout of Sporting Events on T.V.: Hearings*, Rozelle testimony, 59.

12. Ibid., *Chicago Tribune*, 24 December 1972.

13. *New York Times*, 21 December 1972, 45.

14. *Broadcasting*, 9 October 1972, 25.

15. *Blackout of Sporting Events on T.V.: Hearings*, testimony of Don Ruck, 95.

16. Ibid., 90; *Broadcasting*, 9 October 1972, 26.

17. *Blackout of Sporting Events on T.V.: Hearings*, testimony of Walter Kennedy, 84.

18. Ibid., 87.

19. Ibid., testimony of Bowie Kuhn, 131.

20. Ibid.

21. *Broadcasting*, 30 July 1973.

22. Committee on Interstate and Foreign Commerce, United States House of Representatives, 90th Cong., 1st sess. (1973), *Professional Sports Broadcasts*, testimony of Pete Rozelle, 198, "Why Pro Football Insists on TV Blackouts," *U.S. News and World Report*, 75 (10 September 1973), 60–64.

23. *Professional Sports Blackouts*, Rozelle testimony, 188.

24. Ibid., testimony of Bowie Kuhn, 158; *Chicago Tribune*, 6 September 1973.

25. *Professional Sports Blackouts*, testimony of Walter Kennedy, 122; *Broadcasting*, 6 August 1972, 20.

26. *Professional Sports Blackouts*, testimony of Don Ruck, 26.

27. "One For the Home Team," *Newsweek*, 82 (17 September 1973), 79–80.

28. *Broadcasting*, 9 October 1972, 21.

29. *New York Times*, 7, 14 September 1973, 1; *Chicago Tribune*, 7, 14 September 1973.

30. *New York Times*, 14 September 1973, 1.

31. "One For the Home Team," 79–80; Jerry Kirshenbaum, "Chirp-Chirp, Crunch-Crunch" *Sports Illustrated*, 39 (1 October 1973), 38–40.

32. *New York Times*, 13 September 1973, 65.

33. *Chicago Tribune*, 13 September 1973.

34. Ibid., 14 September 1973.

35. *New York Times*, 16 September 1973, IV, 15.

36. Committee on Commerce, United States Senate, 93rd Cong., 2d sess. (1974), *Report of the FCC on the Effect of P.L. 93–107, the Sports Anti-Blackout Law*, 8.

37. Committee on Commerce, United States Senate, 94th Cong. 2d sess. (1976), *Third Annual Report of the FCC on the Effect of P.L. 93–107, the Sports Anti-Blackout Law*, 28.

38. Ibid., 29.

39. Ibid., 40; *Broadcasting*, 22 April 1975, 5.

40. Committee on Commerce, United States Senate, 94th Cong. 1st sess. (1975), *T.V. Blackout of Sporting Events*, testimony of Pete Rozelle, 18.

41. Committee on Interstate and Foreign Commerce, United States House of Representatives, 94th Cong., 1st sess. (1975), *Second Annual Report of the FCC on the Effect of P.L. 93–107, the Sports Anti-Blackout Law*, 82.

42. *T.V. Blackout of Sporting Events*, 41.

43. Committee on Interstate and Foreign Commerce, United States House of Representatives, 94th Cong., 1st sess. (1976), *Sports Broadcasting Act of 1975: Hearings*, 2.

44. *New York Times*, 1 November 1975, 23; "Scorecard," *Sports Illustrated*, 43 (10 November 1975), 18.

45. *New York Times*, 31 October 1975, 39; *Broadcasting*, 3 November 1975, 30.

46. *Sports Broadcasting Act of 1975: Hearings*, 40.

47. *New York Times*, 16 December 1975, 55.

48. Ibid., 19 December 1975, 7; *Broadcasting*, 22 December 1975, 22.

49. *New York Times*, 5 April 1978, 26; *Broadcasting*, 15 December 1975, 26, 3 May 1976, 24–25.

50. *Broadcasting*, 14 June 1976, 25.

51. Ibid., 5 July, 11 October 1976, 32.

52. Ibid., 24 May 1976, 54.

53. Committee on Commerce, Science, and Transportation, United States Senate, 95 Congress, 1 session (1977), *Fourth Annual Report of the FCC on the Effect of P.L. 93–107, the Sports Anti-Blackout Law,* passim; Committee on Commerce, Science, and Transportation, United States Senate, 95 Congress, 2 session (1978), *Fifth Annual Report of the FCC on the Effect of P.L. 93–107, the Sports Anti-Blackout Law.*

54. *Fourth Annual Report of the FCC on the Effect of P.L. 93–107*, 47.

55. *Fifth Annual Report of the FCC on the Effect of P.L. 93–107*, 32.

56. Committee on Interstate and Foreign Commerce, United States House of Representatives, 95th Cong., 2d sess. (1978), *Sports Anti-Blackout Legislation—Oversight,* testimony of Don Shula, 35.

57. Ibid., testimony of Dick Anderson, 35.

58. Ibid., testimony of Joe Robbie, 51.

59. Committee on Judiciary, United States Senate, 101st Cong., 1st sess. (1989), *Sports Programming and Cable Television,* passim; Committee on Energy and Commerce, United States House of Representatives, 101st Cong., 2 sess. (1990), *Cable Television, Part 2,* passim.

60. USA *Today*, 15 October 1989.

61. *Sports Programming and Cable Television*, 1.

62. Ibid., testimonies of Francis Vincent and Paul Tagliabue, 82.

63. Tom McMillen and Paul Coggins, *Out of Bounds: How the American Sports Establishment Is Being Driven by Greed and Hypocrisy— and What Needs to Be Done About It* (New York: Simon and Schuster, 1992), 182, 196–98; Jim Spence and Dave Diles, *Up Close and Personal: The Inside Story of Network Television Sports* (New York: Atheneum, 1988), 340.

64. *Sports Programming and Cable Television,* Tagliabue testimony, 82.

65. McMillen and Coggins, *Out of Bounds*, 200.

66. See John W. Kingdon, *Congressmen's Voting Decisions* (New York: Harper and Row, 1973), 38.

Chapter 8

1. *New York Times*, 9 June 1966, 59.

2. "In A Word, Money," *Time*, 88 (29 July 1966), 34; Lionel Sobel, *Professional Sports and the Law* (New York: Law-Arts, 1977), 383.

3. Jack Horrigan and Mike Rathet, *The Other League* (Chicago: Follett, 1970), 30.

4. Sobel, *Professional Sports and the Law*, 385.

5. Chicago *Tribune*, 21 September 1966; *Sporting News*, 24 September 1966.

6. Committee on Judiciary, United States Senate, 89th Cong., 2d sess. (1966), *Authorizing the Merger of Two or More Professional Football Leagues, and to Protect Football Contests Between Secondary Schools from Professional Football Telecasts, Report on S. 3817.*

7. Chicago *Tribune*, 23 September 1966.

8. *Congressional Record*, 89th Cong., 2d sess., 112 (26 September 1966), 23810.

9. Chicago *Tribune*, 27 September 1966.

10. Letter, Darrel E. Berg to Emanuel Celler, 17 October 1966, Emanuel Celler Papers, Library of Congress, Washington, D.C..

11. Letter, Gary Saymes to Emanuel Celler, 22 September 1966, Ibid.

12. *New York Times*, 7 October 1966, 50.

13. *Chicago Tribune*, 7 October 1966.

14. Ibid., 14 October 1966.

15. Ibid., 15 October 1966; *New York Times*, 15 October 1966, 19.

16. *Washington Post*, 15 October 1966.

17. Ibid.

18. *Congressional Record*, 89th Cong., 2d sess., 112 (20 October 1966), 28231.

19. *Washington Post*, 15 October 1966; Chicago *Tribune*, 21 October 1966.

20. *Congressional Record*, 89th Cong., 2d sess., 112 (20 October 1966), 28230.

21. *Washington Post*, 21 October 1966; Chicago *Tribune*, 22 October 1966.

22. *Congressional Quarterly*, 28 October 1966, 725.

23. *Sporting News*, 5 November 1966.

24. *Congressional Quarterly*, 28 October 1966, 725.

25. *Washington Post*, 21 October 1966.

26. Sobel, *Professional Sports and the Law,* 393; see also, Gary Davidson and Bill Libby, *Breaking the Game Wide Open* (New York: Atheneum, 1974); Glenn Dickey, *The History of Basketball Since 1896* (New York: Stein and Day, 1982); David Halberstam, *The Breaks of the Game* (New York: Alfred A. Knopf, 1981).

27. Sobel, *Professional Sports and the Law*, 395.

28. Frank DeFord, "Dribbling on the Verge of a Merge," *Sports Illustrated*, 34 (9 August 1971), 68; "Basketball's Super Bowl," *Newsweek*, 77 (24 May 1971), 65.

29. *Robertson v. National Basketball Association*, 389 F. Supp. 867 (1975).

30. Paul D. Staudohar, *The Sports Industry and Collective Bargaining* (Ithaca: ILR Press, 1986), 101.

31. Roger G. Noll, "Professional Basketball: Economic and Business Perspectives," in Paul D. Staudohar and James A. Mangan, eds., *The Business of Professional Sports* (Urbana: University of Illinois Press, 1991), 18–47.

32. Letter, Philip Hart to Harvey Campbell, 26 September 1961, Philip Hart Papers, Bentley Historical Library, University of Michigan, Ann Arbor, MI.

33. *Wall Street Journal*, 20 October 1971; *New York Times*, 22 September 1971, 57.

34. Ibid.

35. Subcommittee on Anti-Trust and Monopoly, United States Senate, 92nd Cong., 1st sess. (1971), *Professional Basketball, Part 1*, statement of Senator Sam Ervin, 14–15.

36. Ibid.

37. *Professional Basketball, Part 1*, testimony of Oscar Robertson, 305.

38. Subcommittee on Anti-Trust and Monopoly, United States Senate, 92d Cong., 1st–2d sess. (1971–72), *Professional Basketball, Part 2*, testimony of Bill Bradley, 866.

39. *Professional Basketball, Part 1*, testimony of Lawrence Fleisher, 226; Committee on Judiciary, United States House of Representatives, 92d Cong., 2d sess. (1972), *The Anti-Trust Laws and Professional Team Sports Including Consideration of the Proposed Merger of the American and National Basketball Associations*, testimony of Lawrence Fleisher, 146.

40. Halberstam, *The Breaks of the Game*, 271.

41. *Professional Basketball, Part 2*, testimony of John Mackey, 839; *New York Times*, 7 March 1972, 47.

42. *Professional Basketball, Part 2*, testimony of Ed Garvey, 834; *The Anti-Trust Laws and Professional Team Sports Including Consideration of the Proposed Merger of the American and National Basketball Associations*, testimony of Ed Garvey, 253.

43. *Professional Basketball, Part 1*, testimony of Rick Barry, 146.

44. Ibid., 154.

45. Ibid., testimony of Thomas Kuchel, 92.

46. *The Anti-Trust Laws and Professional Team Sports Including Consideration of the Proposed Merger of the American and National Basketball Associations,* testimony of Thomas Kuchel, 19.

47. Ibid., testimony of Walter Kennedy, 122.

48. *Professional Basketball, Part 2,* testimony of Jack Dolph, 747.

49. "Professional Sports: A Business Boom in Trouble," *U.S. News and World Report,* 71 (5 July 1971), 51.

50. *Professional Basketball, Part 2,* 21.

51. Sobel, *Professional Sports and the Law,* 405.

52. Committee on Judiciary, United States Senate, 92d Cong., 2d sess. (1972), *Authorizing the Merger of Two or More Professional Basketball Leagues, and for Other Purposes, Report,* 6; *Chicago Tribune,* 8 September 1972.

53. *Authorizing the Merger of Two or More Professional Basketball Leagues, and for Other Purposes, Report,* 9.

54. Ibid.

55. *New York Times,* 22 September 1972, 50; *Chicago Tribune,* 16 November 1972.

56. *Washington Post,* 16 September 1976.

57. *Congressional Quarterly,* 28 October 1966, 27; *Sporting News,* 5 November 1966.

58. Roger G. Noll, ed., *Government and the Sport Business* (Washington: Brookings Institution, 1974), 427; Davidson and Libby, *Breaking the Game Wide Open,* 87–88.

Chapter 9

1. Arthur T. Johnson, "The Sports Franchise Relocation Issue and Public Policy Responses," in Arthur T. Johnson and James H. Frey, eds., *Government and Sport: The Public Policy Issues* (Totowa, NJ: Rowman & Allanheld, 1985), 232.

2. Robert Lindsay, "Al Davis Tackles Pro Football," *New York Times Magazine* (13 December 1981), 96.

3. *Los Angeles Memorial Coliseum v. National Football League,* 726 F. 2d 1381 (1984).

4. Randy Roberts and James S. Olson, *Winning Is the Only Thing: Sports in America Since 1945* (Baltimore: Johns Hopkins University Press, 1989), 3; *Washington Post,* 17 September 1982.

5. Committee on Judiciary, United States House of Representatives, 97th Cong., 1–2 sess. (1981–82), *Anti-Trust and Professional Sports,* 181, 506–10.

6. Committee on Judiciary, United States Senate, *Professional Sports and the Anti-Trust Laws*, 97th Cong., 2d sess. (1982), *Professional Sports Anti-Trust Immunity*, testimony of Pete Rozelle, 26; *New York Times*, 1 October 1982, 11; *Washington Post*, 1 October 1982.

7. *Professional Sports and the Anti-Trust Laws*, 46.

8. Howard Cosell, *I Never Played the Game* (New York: William Morrow, 1985), 104.

9. *Professional Sports and the Anti-Trust Laws*, testimony of Al Davis, 310.

10. Ibid., 324.

11. Ibid., 312; *Washington Post*, 21 September 1982.

12. *Professional Sports and the Anti-Trust Laws*, testimony of Ed Garvey, 88; *New York Times*, 1 October 1982, 11; *Washington Post*, 1 October 1982.

13. *Professional Sports and the Anti-Trust Laws*, testimony of Gene Upshaw, 116.

14. *USA Today*, 21 September 1982.

15. *Anti-Trust and Professional Sports*, testimony of Howard Cosell; *Washington Post*, 17 July 1982; Cosell, *I Never Played the Game*, 96.

16. *USA Today*, 17 September 1982.

17. *Los Angeles Memorial Coliseum v. National Football League*, 726 F. 2d 1381 (1984).

18. Committee on Energy and Commerce, United States House of Representatives, 99th Cong., 1st sess. (1985), *Professional Sports*, 2.

19. *New York Times*, 19 January 1985, 27.

20. *Washington Post*, 5, 20 February 1985; *USA Today*, 7 February 1985.

21. Committee on Commerce Science and Transportation, United States Senate, 99th Cong., 1st sess. (1985), *Sports Community Protection Act of 1985*, 47.

22. Ibid., testimony of Pete Rozelle, 64; Committee on Commerce, Science, and Transportation, United States Senate, 98th Cong., 2d sess. (1984), *Professional Sports Team Community Protection Act, Hearings*, testimony of Pete Rozelle, 63.

23. *Sports Community Protection Act of 1985*, Rozelle testimony, 63; *New York Times*, 5 February 1985, II, 7.

24. Senate, *Professional Sports Team Community Protection Act, Hearings*, testimony of James Fitzpatrick, 73.

25. *Professional Team Sports*, testimony of Philip Hochberg, 143; Senate, *Professional Sports Team Community Protection Act, Hearings*, 152.

26. Senate, *Professional Sports Team Community Protection Act, Hearings*, 156.

27. Committee on Energy and Commerce, United States House of Representatives, 98th Cong., 2d sess. (1984), *Professional Sports Team Community Protection Act, Hearings*, 9.

28. Ibid., testimony of Donald Schaefer, 31.

29. Ibid., 32; *Washington Post*, 21 February 1985.

30. Senate, *Professional Sports Team Community Protection Act, Hearings*, testimony of Gene Upshaw, 94.

31. *Sports Community Protection Act of 1985*, testimony of Donald Fehr, 139–40.

32. Ibid., 1.

33. Robert C. Berry, William B. Gould, and Paul D. Staudohar, *Labor Relations in Professional Sports* (Dover: Auburn House, 1986), 256.

Conclusion

1. Committee on Interstate and Foreign Commerce, United States Senate, 83d Cong., 1st sess. (1953), *Broadcasting and Televising Baseball Games: Hearings on S. 1396*, statement of Edwin C. Johnson, 4.

Bibliography

Archival Resources

Emanuel Celler Papers, Library of Congress, Washington, D.C.

Philip Hart Papers, Bentley Historical Library, University of Michigan, Ann Arbor.

Kenneth Keating Papers, Rush Rhees Library, University of Rochester, Rochester.

Estes Kefauver Papers, Special Collections, Hoskins Library, University of Tennessee, Knoxville.

Government Documents

U.S. Congress. House. Committee on Interstate and Foreign Commerce. *Prohibition of Interstate Transportation of Pictures and Descriptions of Prizefights and the Nullification of the State Anti-Gambling Laws.* 61st Cong., 2d-3d sess., 1910–1911.

U.S. Congress. House. Committee on Interstate and Foreign Commerce. *Interstate Transportation of Pictures of Prizefights, Report.* 62d Cong., 2d sess., 1912.

U.S. Congress. Senate. Committee on Interstate Commerce. *Legalizing Transportation of Prize-Fight Films.* 76th Cong., 1st sess., 1939.

U.S. Congress. Committee on Interstate Commerce. *Divesting Prize-Fight Films of Their Interstate Character.* 76th Cong., 1st sess., 1939.

U.S. Congress. House. Committee on Interstate and Foreign Commerce. *Divesting Prize-Fight Films of Their Character as Subjects of Interstate and Foreign Commerce.* 73d Cong. 3d sess., 1940.

U.S. Congress. House. Subcommittee on the Study of Monopoly Power. *Organized Baseball, Part 6.* 82d Cong., 1st sess., 1951.

U.S. Congress. House. Committee on Judiciary. *Organized Baseball: Report of the Subcommittee on the Study of Monopoly Power of Committee on Judiciary pursuant to H.R. 95.* 82d Cong. 2d sess., 1952.

U.S. Congress. Senate. Committee on Interstate and Foreign Commerce. *Broadcasting and Televising Baseball Games: Hearings on S. 1396.* 83d Cong., 1st sess., 1953.

U.S. Congress. Senate. Committee on Interstate and Foreign Commerce. *Report from Committee on Judiciary and Foreign Commerce to accompany S. 1396.* 83d Cong., 1st sess., 1953.

U.S. Congress. Senate. Committee on Judiciary. *Subjecting Professional Baseball Clubs to Anti-Trust Laws: Hearings on S.J. 133.* 83d Cong., 2d sess., 1954.

U.S. Congress. House. Committee on Judiciary. *Organized Professional Team Sports: Hearings.* 85th Cong., 1st sess., 1957.

U.S. Congress. House. Committee on Judiciary. *Applicability of Anti-Trust Laws to Organized Professional Team Sports Report on H.R. 10378.* 85th Cong., 2d sess., 1958.

U.S. Congress. House. Committee on Judiciary. *Consideration of Bill to Limit Applicability of Anti-Trust Laws Relative to Designated Professional Team Sports.* 85th Cong., 2d sess., 1958.

U.S. Congress. Senate. Committee on Judiciary. *Organized Professional Team Sports: Hearings before Subcommittee on Anti-Trust Laws and Monopoly Pursuant to S. 231 on H.R. 10378.* 85th Cong., 2d sess., 1958.

U.S. Congress. Senate. Committee on Judiciary. *Organized Professional Team Sports: Hearings before Subcommittee on Anti-Trust and Monopoly.* 86th Cong., 1st sess., 1959.

U.S. Congress. Senate. Committee on Judiciary. *Organized Professional Team Sports, 1960: Hearings before Subcommittee on Anti-Trust and Monopoly, pursuant to S. 238.* 86th Cong., 2d sess., 1960.

U.S. Congress. Senate. Committee on Judiciary. *Report on Professional Sports Anti-Trust Act of 1960.* 86th Cong., 2d sess., 1960.

U.S. Congress. Senate. Committee on Judiciary. *Professional Boxing. Part 1: Jacob "Jake" LaMotta.* 86th Cong., 2d sess., 1960.

U.S. Congress. Senate. Committee on Judiciary. *Professional Boxing. Part 2: Frank Carbo.* 86th Cong., 2d sess., 1960.

U.S. Congress. Senate. Committee on Judiciary. *Professional Boxing. Part 3.* 87th Cong., 1st sess., 1961.

U.S. Congress. House. Committee on Judiciary. *Telecasting of Professional Sports Contests: Hearings before Anti-Trust Subcommittee.* 87th Cong., 1st sess., 1961.

U.S. Congress. House. Committee on Judiciary. *Telecasting of Professional Sports Contests: Report on H.R. 9096.* 87th Cong., 1st sess., 1961.

U.S. Congress. Senate. Committee on Judiciary. *Telecasting of Professional Sports Contests.* 87th Cong., 1st sess., 1961.

U.S. Congress. Senate. Committee on Judiciary. *Report on H.R. 9096.* 87th Cong., 1st sess., 1961.

U.S. Congress. Senate. Committee on Judiciary. *Bribery in Sports Contests.* 87th Cong., 2d sess., 1962.

U.S. Congress. House. Committee on Judiciary. *Bribery in Sporting Contests.* 88th Cong., 1st sess., 1963.

U.S. Congress. Senate. Committee on Judiciary. *Bribery in Sporting Contests.* 88th Cong., 1st sess., 1963.

U.S. Congress. Senate. Committee on Judiciary. *Professional Boxing. Part 4: Liston-Clay Fight.* 88th Cong., 2d sess., 1964.

U.S. Congress. Senate. Committee on Judiciary. *Professional Sports Anti-Trust Bill: 1964.* 88th Cong., 2d sess., 1964.

U.S. Congress. Senate. Committee on Judiciary. *Applicability of the Anti-Trust Laws to Certain Aspects of Designated Organized Professional Team Sports.* 88th Cong., 2d sess., 1964.

U.S. Congress. House. Committee on Interstate and Foreign Commerce. *Federal Boxing Commission, Hearings.* 89th Cong., 1st sess., 1965.

U.S. Congress. House. Committee on Interstate and Foreign Commerce. *Federal Boxing Commission.* 89th Cong., 1st sess., 1965.

U.S. Congress. Senate. Committee on Judiciary. *Professional Sports Anti-Trust Bill, 1965: Hearings before Subcommittee on Anti-Trust and Monopoly.* 89th Cong., 1st sess., 1965.

U.S. Congress. Senate. Committee on Judiciary. *Professional Sports Act of 1965: Report on S. 950.* 89th Cong., 1st sess., 1965.

U.S. Congress. House. Committee of Conference. *Suspensions of Investment Credit Accelerated Depreciation: Conference Report to Accompany H.R. 17607.* 89th Cong., 2d sess., 1966.

U.S. Congress. Senate. Committee on Judiciary. *Authorizing the Merger of Two or More Professional Football Leagues, and to Protect Football Contests Between Secondary Schools from Professional Football Telecasts, Report on S. 3817.* 89th Cong., 2d sess., 1966.

U.S. Congress. Senate. Committee on Judiciary. *Professional Basketball. Part 1.* 92d Cong., 1st sess., 1971.

U.S. Congress. House. Committee on Judiciary. *The Anti-Trust Laws and Professional Team Sports Including Consideration of the Proposed Merger of the American and National Basketball Associations.* 92d Cong., 2d sess., 1972.

U.S. Congress. Senate. Committee on Commerce. *Federal Sports Act of 1972, Hearings.* 92d Cong., 2d sess., 1972.

U.S. Congress. Senate. Committee on Communication. *Blackout of Sporting Events on T.V.: Hearings on S. 4007 and S. 4010.* 92d Cong., 2d sess., 1972.

U.S. Congress. Senate. Committee on Judiciary. *Professional Basketball. Part 2.* 92d Cong., 2d sess., 1972.

U.S. Congress. Senate. Committee on Judiciary. *Authorizing the Merger of Two or More Professional Basketball Leagues, and for Other Purposes.* 92d Cong., 2d sess., 1972.

U.S. Congress. House. Committee on Interstate and Foreign Commerce. *Evaluation of the Necessity for Television Blackouts of Professional Sporting Events.* 93d Cong., 1st sess., 1973.

U.S. Congress. House. Committee on Interstate and Foreign Commerce. *Professional Sports—T.V. Blackouts.* 93d Cong., 1st sess., 1973.

U.S. Congress. House. Committee on Interstate and Foreign Commerce. *Professional Sports Blackouts.* 93d Cong., 1st sess., 1973.

U.S. Congress. Senate. Committee on Commerce. *T.V. Blackout—Professional Sports.* 93d Cong., 1st sess., 1973.

U.S. Congress. Senate. Committee on Communication. *Report of the FCC on the Effect of P.L. 93–107, the Sports Anti-Blackout Law.* 93d Cong., 2d sess., 1974.

U.S. Congress. House. Committee on Interstate and Foreign Commerce. *Second Annual Report of the FCC on the Effect of P.L. 93–107, the Sports Anti-Blackout Law.* 94th Cong., 1st sess., 1975.

U.S. Congress. House. Committee on Interstate and Foreign Commerce. *Sports Broadcasting Act of 1975.* 94th Cong., 1st sess., 1975.

U.S. Congress. House. Committee on Judiciary. *Rights of Professional Athletes.* 94th Cong., 1st sess., 1975.

U.S. Congress. Senate. Committee on Commerce. *T.V. Blackout of Sporting Events.* 94th Cong., 1st sess., 1975.

U.S. Congress. House. Committee on Interstate and Foreign Commerce. *Sports Broadcasting Act of 1975: Hearings.* 94th Cong., 2d sess., 1976.

U.S. Congress. Senate. Committee on Commerce. *Third Annual Report of the FCC on the Effect of P.L. 93–107, the Sports Anti-Blackout Law.* 94th Cong., 2d sess., 1976.

U.S. Congress. House. Select Committee on Professional Sports. *Inquiry Into Professional Sports, Part 1.* 94th Cong., 2d sess., 1976.

U.S. Congress. House. Select Committee on Professional Sports. *Inquiry Into Professional Sports, Part 2.* 94th Cong., 2d sess., 1976.

U.S. Congress. House. Select Committee on Professional Sports. *Professional Sports and the Law.* 94th Cong., 2d sess., 1976.

U.S. Congress. House. Select Committee on Professional Sports. *Inquiry Into Professional Sports: Final Meetings.* 94th Cong., 2d sess., 1976–1977.

U.S. Congress. House. Select Committee on Professional Sports. *Inquiry Into Professional Sports: Final Report of the Select Committee on Professional Sports.* 94th Cong., 2d sess., 1977.

U.S. Congress. Senate. Committee on Commerce, Science, and Transportation. *Fourth Annual Report of the FCC on the Effect of P.L. 93–107, the Sports Anti-Blackout Law.* 95th Cong., 1st sess., 1977.

U.S. Congress. House. Committee on Interstate and Foreign Commerce. *Sports Anti-Blackout Legislation—Oversight*. 95th Cong., 2d sess., 1978.

U.S. Congress. Senate. Committee on Commerce, Science, and Transportation. *Fifth Annual Report of the FCC on the Effect of P.L. 93–107, the Sports Anti-Blackout Law*. 95th Cong., 2d sess., 1978.

U.S. Congress. House. Committee on Education and Labor. *Hearings on the Creation of a Federal Boxing Board*. 96th Cong., 1st sess., 1979.

U.S. Congress. House. Committee on Judiciary. *Anti-Trust Policy and Professional Sports*. 97th Cong., 1st–2d sess., 1981–1982.

U.S. Congress. Senate. Committee on Judiciary. *Professional Sports Anti-Trust Immunity*. 97th Cong., 2d sess., 1982.

U.S. Congress. House. Committee on Education and Labor. *Congressional Advisory Commission on Boxing*. 98th Cong., 1st sess., 1983.

U.S. Congress. House. Committee on Energy and Commerce. *Boxing Reform, Hearings*. 98th Cong., 1st sess., 1983.

U.S. Congress. House. Committee on Energy and Commerce. *Congressional Advisory Commission on Boxing, Report*. 98th Cong., 1st sess., 1983.

U.S. Congress. House. Committee on Energy and Commerce. *Professional Sports Team Community Protection Act: Hearings*. 98th Cong., 2d sess., 1984.

U.S. Congress. Senate. Committee on Commerce, Science, and Transportation. *Professional Sports Team Community Protection Act: Hearings*. 98th Cong., 2d sess., 1984.

U.S. Congress. Senate. Committee on Commerce, Science, and Transportation. *Professional Sports Team Community Protection Act: Report*. 98th Cong., 2d sess., 1984.

U.S. Congress. House. Committee on Energy and Commerce. *Professional Sports*. 99th Cong., 1st sess., 1985.

U.S. Congress. Senate. Committee on Commerce, Science, and Transportation. *Sports Community Protection Act of 1985*. 99th Cong., 1st sess., 1985.

U.S. Congress. Senate. Committee on Commerce, Science, and Transportation. *Professional Sports Communication Act of 1985, Report*. 99th Cong., 1st sess., 1985.

U.S. Congress. Senate. Committee on Judiciary. *Professional Sports Anti-Trust Immunity*. 99th Cong., 1st sess., 1985.

U.S. Congress. Senate. Committee on Judiciary. *Anti-Trust Implications of the Recent NFL Television Contract*. 100th Cong., 1st sess., 1987.

U.S. Congress. Senate. Committee on Judiciary. *Sports Programming and Cable Television*. 101st Cong., 1st sess., 1989.

U.S. Congress. House. Committee on Energy and Commerce. *Cable Television Regulation*. 101st Cong., 2d sess., 1990.

Congressional Record 61st–98th Congress.

Court Cases

Federal Baseball Club v. National League 259 U.S. 200 (1922).

Gardella v. Chandler 79 F. Supp. 260 (1948).

Toolson v. New York Yankees 346 U.S. 356 (1953).

U.S. v. National Football League 116 F. Supp. 319 (1953).

U.S. v. International Boxing Club 348 U.S. 236 (1955).

Radovich v. National Football League 352 U.S. 445 (1957).

U.S. v. National Football League 196 F. Supp. 445 (1961).

Flood v. Kuhn et al. 407 U.S. 258 (1972).

Kapp v. National Football League 390 F. Supp. 73 (1974).

Robertson v. National Basketball Association 389 F. Supp. 867 (1975).

Mackey v. National Football League 543 F. 2d 606 (1976).

Los Angeles Memorial Coliseum v. National Football League 726 F. 2d 1381 (1984).

Newspapers

Broadcasting 1953–78.

Chicago Tribune 1966–90.

Congressional Quarterly 1965–79.

New York Times 1951–93.

Sporting News 1951–78.

Wall Street Journal 1970–93.

Washington Post 1951–93.

USA Today 1980–93.

Books

Alexander, Charles C. *Our Game: An American Baseball History*. New York: Henry Holt, 1991.

___. *Ty Cobb*. New York: Oxford University Press, 1984.

Allison, Dean B., and Bruce B. Henderson. *Empire of Deceit*. Garden City: Doubleday, 1985.

Anderson, Jack, and Fred Blumenthal. *The Kefauver Story*. New York: Dial Press, 1956.

Berry, Robert C., and Glenn M. Wong. *Law and the Business of Professional Sports Leagues*. 2 vols. Dover: Auburn House, 1986.

Berry, Robert C., William B. Gould, and Paul D. Staudohar. *Labor Relations in Professional Sports*. Dover: Auburn House, 1986.

Cantelon, Hart, and Richard Gruneau, eds. *Sport, Culture, and the Modern State*. Toronto: University of Toronto Press, 1982.

Celler, Emanuel. *You Never Leave Brooklyn: The Autobiography of Emanuel Celler*. New York: John Day, 1953.

Chandler, Joan. *Television and National Sport: The United States and Great Britain*. Urbana: University of Illinois Press, 1988.

Clausen, Aage R. *How Congressmen Decide: A Policy Focus*. New York: St. Martin's Press, 1973.

Cobb, Ty. *My Life in Baseball: The True Record*. New York: Doubleday, 1961.

Cosell, Howard. *Cosell*. Chicago: Playboy Press, 1973.

___. *I Never Played the Game*. New York: William Morrow, 1985.

___. *Like It Is*. Chicago: Playboy Press, 1974.

Creamer, Robert W. *Stengel: His Life and Times*. New York: Simon and Schuster, 1984.

Davidson, Gary, and Bill Libby. *Breaking the Game Wide Open*. New York: Atheneum, 1974.

Davidson, Roger H., and Walter J. Oleszek. *Congress Against Itself*. Bloomington: Indiana University Press, 1977.

Dickey, Glenn. *The History of Professional Basketball Since 1896*. New York: Stein and Day, 1982.

Durso, Joseph. *The All-American Dollar: The Big-Business of Sports*. Boston: Houghton Mifflin, 1971.

Dworkin, James B. *Owners Versus Players: Baseball and Collective Bargaining*. Boston: Auburn House, 1981.

Feller, Bob. *Now Pitching*. New York: Harper Collins, 1990.

Fenno, Richard F., Jr. *Congressmen in Committees*. Boston: Little, Brown, 1973.

Fontenay, Charles L. *Estes Kefauver: A Biography*. Knoxville: University of Tennessee Press, 1980.

Freedman, Warren. *Professional Sports and Anti-Trust*. New York: Quorum Books, 1987.

Goodwin, George, Jr. *The Little Legislatures: Committees of Congress*. Amherst: University of Massachusetts Press, 1970.

Gorman, Joseph Bruce. *Estes Kefauver: A Political Biography*. New York: Oxford University Press, 1971.

Gray, Ronald. *Congressional Television: A Legislative History*. Westport: Greenwood Press, 1984.

Guttmann, Allen. *A Whole New Ball Game: An Interpretation of American Sports*. Chapel Hill: University of North Carolina Press, 1988.

___. *From Ritual to Record: The Nature of Modern Sports*. New York: Columbia University Press, 1978.

Halberstam, David. *The Breaks of the Game.* New York: Albert A. Knopf, 1981.

Hamilton, James. *The Power to Probe: A Study of Congressional Investigations.* New York: Random House, 1976.

Harris, David. *The League: The Rise and Fall of the NFL.* New York: Bantam Books, 1986.

Heller, Peter. *"In This Corner . . . !" Forty World Champions Tell Their Stories.* New York: Simon and Schuster, 1973.

Horrigan, Jack, and Mike Rathet. *The Other League.* Chicago: Follet, 1970.

Johnson, Arthur T., and James H. Frey. *Government and Sport: The Public Policy Issues.* Totowa: Rowman and Allanheld, 1985.

Johnson, William O., Jr. *Super Spectator and the Electric Lilliputians.* Boston: Little, Brown, 1971.

Kefauver, Estes. *Crime In America.* Garden City: Doubleday 1951.

____. *In a Few Hands: Monopoly Power in America.* New York: Pantheon Books, 1965.

Kefauver, Estes, and Jack Levin. *A Twentieth Century Congress.* New York: Greenwood Press, 1969.

Kingdon, John W. *Congressmen's Voting Decisions.* New York: Harper and Row, 1973.

Lipsky, Richard. *Why We Play the Game: Why Sports Dominate American Life.* Boston: Beacon Press, 1981.

Louis, Joe. *My Life Story.* New York: Duell, Sloan and Pierce, 1947.

Lowenfish, Lee, and Tony Lupien. *The Imperfect Diamond.* New York: Stein and Day, 1980.

McMillen, Tom, and Paul Coggins. *Out of Bounds: How the American Sports Establishment Is Being Driven by Greed and Hypocrisy—and What Needs to Be Done About It.* New York: Simon and Schuster, 1992.

Mandell, Richard D. *Sport: A Cultural History.* New York: Columbia University Press, 1984.

Mann, Thomas E., and Norman J. Ornstein. *The New Congress.* Washington, D.C.: American Enterprise Institute for Public Policy Research, 1981.

Matthews, Donald R., and James A. Stimson. *Yeas and Neas: Normal Decision Making in the U.S. House of Representatives.* New York: John Wiley and Sons, 1975.

Mead, Chris. *Champion Joe Louis: Black Hero in White America.* New York: Charles Scribner's Sons, 1985.

Morrow, William L. *Congressional Committees.* New York: Charles Scribner's Sons, 1969.

Murdock, Eugene C. *Ban Johnson: Czar of Baseball*. Westport: Greenwood Press, 1982.

Nagler, Barney. *James Norris and the Decline of Boxing*. Indianapolis: Bobbs-Merrill, 1964.

Noll, Roger G., ed., *Government and the Sport Business*. Washington, D.C.: Brookings Institution, 1974.

Obojski, Robert. *Bush League: A History of Minor League Baseball*. New York: Macmillan, 1975.

Parker, Glenn R., and Suzanne L. Parker. *Factions in House Committees*. Knoxville: University of Tennessee Press, 1985.

Parrott, Harold. *The Lords of Baseball*. New York: Praeger, 1976.

Powers, Ron. *Supertube: The Rise of Television Sports*. New York: Coward-McCann, 1984.

Rader, Benjamin G. *American Sports: From the Age of Folk Games to the Age of Spectators*. Englewood Cliffs: Prentice-Hall, 1983.

___. *In Its Own Image: How Television Has Transformed Sports*. New York: Macmillan, 1984.

Reid, T.R. *Congressional Odyssey: The Saga of a Senate Bill*. San Francisco: W.H. Freeman, 1980.

Riess, Steven A., ed. *The American Sporting Experience: A Historical Anthology of Sport in America*. New York: Leisure Press, 1984.

Roberts, Randy. *Jack Dempsey: The Manassa Mauler*. Baton Rouge: Louisiana State University Press, 1979.

___. *Papa Jack: Jack Johnson and the Era of White Hopes*. London: Macmillan, 1983.

Roberts, Randy, and James S. Olson. *Winning Is the Only Thing: Sports in America Since 1945*. Baltimore: Johns Hopkins University Press, 1989.

Robinson, Jackie. *I Never Had It Made*. New York: G.P. Putnam's Sons, 1972.

Sammons, Jeffrey T. *Beyond the Ring: The Role of Boxing in American Society*. Chicago: University of Illinois Press, 1988.

Schapsmeier, Edward L., and Frederick H. Schapsmeier. *Dirksen of Illinois: Senatorial Statesman*. Chicago: University of Illinois Press, 1985.

Schuck, Peter H. *The Judiciary Committees*. New York: Grossman 1975.

Seidel, Michael. *Ted Williams: A Baseball Life*. Chicago: Contemporary Books, 1991.

Seymour, Harold. *Baseball*. vols. 1 and 2. New York: Oxford University Press, 1971.

Sheed, Wilfrid. *Muhammad Ali*. New York: Crowell, 1975.

Sobel, Lionel S. *Professional Sports and the Law*. New York: Law-Arts, 1977.

Smith, Steven S., and Christopher J. Deering. *Committees in Congress*. Washington, D.C.: Congressional Quarterly Press, 1990.

Spence, Jim, and Dave Diles. *Up Close and Personal: The Inside Story of Network Television Sports*. New York: Atheneum, 1988.

Staudohar, Paul D. *The Sports Industry and Collective Bargaining*. Ithaca: ILR Press, 1986.

Staudohar, Paul D., and James A. Mangan, eds. *The Business of Professional Sports*. Urbana: University of Illinois Press, 1991.

Sugar, Bert Randolph. *The Thrill of Victory: The Inside Story of ABC Sports*. New York: Hawthorne Books, 1978.

Sullivan, Neil J. *The Dodgers Move West*. New York: Oxford University Press, 1987.

___. *The Minors*. New York: St. Martin's Press, 1990.

Talamini, John T., and Charles S. Page, eds. *Sport and Society: An Anthology*. Boston: Little, Brown, 1973.

Truman, David B. *The Governmental Process*. New York: Alfred A. Knopf, 1963.

Tygiel, Jules. *Baseball's Great Experiment: Jackie Robinson and His Legacy*. New York: Vintage Books, 1983.

Voigt, David Q. *America Through Baseball*. Chicago: Nelson-Hall, 1976.

___. *American Baseball: From Post-War Expansion to the Electronic Age*. vol. 3. University Park: Pennsylvania State University Press, 1983.

Warfield, Don. *The Roaring Redhead: Larry MacPhail, Baseball's Great Innovator*. South Bend: Diamond Communications, 1987.

Wilson, Woodrow. *Congressional Government: A Study in American Politics*. Reprint, New York: World, 1956.

Journal and Magazine Articles

"Aid for Ailing Minors." *Business Week* 16 May 1953: 29.

"Are Ballplayers Slaves?" *U.S. News and World Report* 31 (3 August 1951): 21.

"Baseball Faces Squeeze Play." *Business Week* 11 August 1951: 23.

"Baseball Fights the Anti-Trust Laws." *Business Week* 29 June 1957: 46–47.

"Basketball's Super Bowl." *Newsweek* 77 (24 May 1971): 65.

"Big Sellout—CBS Buys Yankees." *Sports Illustrated* 21 (24 August 1964): 8, 12–17.

"Big Week for Boxing." *Sports Illustrated* 23 (30 August 1965): 7.

"Bootleg T.V." *Sports Illustrated* 17 (12 November 1962): 6–8.

Boyle, Robert H. "Taking Stock of Sonny." *Sports Illustrated* 20 (6 April 1964): 24–27.

"Brinkley vs. the Brontosaurus." *Sports Illustrated* 20 (4 May 1964): 16.

"Bush League Baseball on the Rocks." *Business Week* 14 August 1954: 90.

"Business of Baseball." *Nation* 186 (19 April 1958): 340–43.

DeFord, Frank. "Dribbling on the Verge of a Merge." *Sports Illustrated* 34 (9 August 1971): 68.

French, Burton L. "Subcommittees of Congress." *American Political Science Review* 9 (February 1915): 68–92.

Garvey, Edward R. "From Chattel to Employee: The Athlete's Quest for Freedom and Dignity." *Annals of American Academy of Political and Social Science* 445 (September 1979): 91–101.

Goodwin, George, Jr. "Subcommittees: The Miniature Legislatures of Congress." *American Political Science Review* 56 (September 1962): 596–604.

"Heads, Not Headlines." *Sports Illustrated* 13 (5 December 1960): 12.

Huitt, Ralph K. "The Congressional Committee: A Case Study." *American Political Science Review* 48 (June 1954): 340–65.

"In a Word, Money." *Time* 88 (29 July 1966): 34.

Johnson, Arthur T. "Congress and Professional Sports, 1951–1978." *Annals of the American Academy of Political and Social Science* 445 (September 1979): 102–15.

Jones, Charles O. "The Role of the Congressional Subcommittee." *Midwest Journal of Political Science* 6 (November 1962): 327–44.

Kahn, Roger. "The Yankees: Descent from Olympus." *Saturday Evening Post* 237 (12 September 1964): 80–83.

Kane, Martin. "Estes vs. the Hoods." *Sports Illustrated* 13 (26 December 1960): 28

Kirshenbaum, Jerry. "Chirp-Chirp, Crunch-Crunch." *Sports Illustrated* 39 (1 October 1973): 38–40.

Lardner, John. "Federal Love." *Newsweek* 52 (11 August 1958): 84.

___. "If It Is a Business." *Newsweek* 49 (8 April 1957): 103.

Leggett, William. "Baseball: 1965—Immutable, But Changing." *Sports Illustrated* 22 (19 April 1965): 43–44.

___. "The 28-Million-Dollar Deal." *Sports Illustrated* 20 (3 February 1964): 16–17.

Lindsay, Robert. "Al Davis Tackles Professional Football." *New York Times Magazine* (13 December 1991): 96.

Lundberg, George. "Boxing Should Be Banned in Civilized Societies." *Journal of the American Medical Association* 249 (14 January 1983): 250.

Massaquoi, Hans. "Should Boxing Be Abolished?" *Ebony* 17 (June 1962): 44–46.

"Mr. Gray's Eminence." *Newsweek* 56 (19 December 1960): 64.

"My Co-operation." *Newsweek* 82 (1 October 1973): 64.

"On the 50-Yard Line, 75 Miles from the Game." *Business Week* 5 January 1963: 24–25.

"One For the Home Team." *Newsweek* 82 (17 September 1973): 79–80.

"Only One Thing To Say." *Newsweek* 56 (26 December 1960): 37.

Perkins, Lynette P. "Member Recruitment to a Mixed Goal Committee: The House Judiciary Committee." *Journal of Politics* 43 (May 1981): 349–64.

"Pro Sports: A Business Boom in Trouble." *U.S. News and World Report* 71 (5 July 1971): 56.

Rogin, Gilbert. "Norris' Last Stand." *Sports Illustrated* 13 (19 December 1960): 12–15.

Ruhl, Arthur. "The Fight in the Desert." *Collier's* 45 (23 July 1910): 12–13.

"Runyon with Romance." *Time* 76 (19 December 1960): 43.

"Shape of Things." *Nation* 173 (11 August 1951): 103.

"Sonny and Co." *Time* 83 (10 April 1964): 88.

"Sparring." *Newsweek* 63 (13 April 1964): 63.

"Television Tilts the Old Ball Game." *Life* 57 (28 August 1964): 87–88.

"Theater of the Absurd." *Time* 85 (4 June 1965): 68–69

"The True Picture." *Sports Illustrated* 72 (7 June 1965): 12

"Why Congress Is Taking a Look at Big-Time Sports." *U.S. News and World Report* 45 (18 July 1958): 53.

"Why Pro Football Insists on T.V. Blackouts." *U.S. News and World Report* 75 (10 September 1973): 60–64.

Index

173